Blooming Meadows

The World of Irish Traditional Musicians

TOWN
HOUSE
DUBLIN

Blooming Meadows

The World of Irish Traditional Musicians

Fintan Vallely & Charlie Piggott

Photography by Nutan

First published in 1998
by
Town House and Country House
Trinity House, Charleston Rd
Ranelagh, Dublin 6

ISBN:

Copyright © Photos: Nutan; Text: Fintan Vallely and Charlie Piggott

A CIP catalogue record for this book is available from the
British Library

Typeset by Typeform Repro, Dublin
Printed in Italy by L.E.G.O.

Cover: Miriam Collins

Contents

Introduction

One Sunday morning after a welcome home party for Joe Heaney in O'Donoghue's of Merrion Row, somebody 'borrowed' a bar stool from the pub and took it to the Green, where we were all singing and drinking and lying in the sun. As the stool was left in the park when the light grew dim, I took it home to my bed-and-breakfast in Ormond Quay that night.

I have somehow managed to keep it for the last 31 years and, when Charlie Piggott and I were discussing the idea for this book, I took a notion to photograph everyone on the stool. As Joe Boske describes it with gusto, it is surely the favourite item of public furniture of the traditional music community. I wanted my subjects to be the foreground and the photography to be kept to the background, although faithful to every one of them. I have therefore tended to photograph them at home or in their usual surroundings, using the minimum of photographic paraphernalia.

I used the same film, same camera, same format throughout. I hope I have succeeded in respecting the individual uniqueness of all my 'sitters'. I thank them all for having allowed me into their home, for their time, for the teas, tarts, sandwiches, Jameson and Paddy. They are all utterly different, like each grain of sand on a beach, yet they are all part of the same family. . . The same hum rings through them all, although every bell is different. I hope I have been out of the way, just enough, to let you hear the musical ripples of their beauty.

I have very special thanks for Lucy Farr. Travelling to Berkshire in England where she now lives, chair strapped across my shoulders, was great *craic*. She was so delighted for the visit and she said: 'Honoured to be asked. I am such an ordinary unknown fiddle player.' She played for me every tune we loved, and we danced a bit in the kitchen. She made a delicious chicken casserole, and talked endlessly of everyone we knew. The 'absence of Ireland' all around her in Berkshire made what makes Irish traditional music so special utterly alive.

Lucy said that Joe Cooley had told her once that 'Irish traditional music is the only thing that brings people to their senses.' On leaving her and travelling back through the suburban greyness of London, Lucy and Joe's words shone like beacons of light. She is a very special lady and memories of my visit to her bring tears to my eyes. May she, as she likes to say, live through the millennium and well past it. Thank you Lucy.

NUTAN

The first time ever I heard the sound of a melodeon was when my parents purchased a ten-keyed Hohner for my fourth birthday. While my father tried the instrument with some Kerry polkas, unaware of my presence outside, I stood at the garden gate listening to what I thought was a most magical sound. I was hooked, or should I say trapped, and Irish traditional music has ever since been my ruling passion.

This music is old, as evidenced by many references in the ancient literature. In Ireland, as in other European countries like Greece and Sweden, the tradition runs unbroken today. In the national repertoire there exist some ten to twelve thousand melodies, many more having been irretrievably lost.

When referring to traditional music, tunes and melodies always hold a pivotal position. Everything else is subsidiary, musicians simply acting as mediums or carriers, enabling the music to pass from one generation to the next. Traditional music may be distinguished from other types of music like jazz, popular, classical or art music by its archaic primal or elemental nature and any attempt — for whatever reason — to diminish this nature lessens the power of the music for future generations.

It has always been my experience that a sense of fun and merriment accompanies traditional music. During sessions, between sets of jigs, reels, hornpipes or polkas, musicians spin yarns or stories which aid the 'lifting' of succeeding melodies and so on. The Clare piper Michael Falsey related a story during a session once, illustrating the fact that many of the older musicians of past generations, besides playing music, depended on their wits for survival. An itinerant concertina player who hadn't eaten for several days was asked to play at a country house-dance on a certain Good Friday night. Half a cured pig hung beside the fireplace and, hoping to be entertained with some nourishing food, he was shocked and amazed when presented with a frugal meal of brown bread and tea: the partaking of animal flesh on the holy day was taboo for all concerned. Unable to contain himself, the musician jumped to his feet and, cutting a portion from the porcine carcass, announced that he had often heard of a fast day but had never heard of a fast night, thereby justifiying his carnivorous undertaking.

Sometimes the stories may refer to tune titles. There's a fine three-part jig in O'Neill's collection entitled 'Tell Her I Am'. The virtuoso Sligo fiddle player Michael Coleman was performing in New York city once, when a female admirer directed her companion towards him to enquire if he was married or not. 'Tell her I am,' was his reply. Joe Cooley also loved to play this jig. He learned it from the box playing of John Kelly from Kilkenny while living in Dublin in the late 1940s. To amuse himself during long winter nights he often asked his flatmate to remind him of the name of the new tune he had learned. The amusing reply with the improperly understood title, 'Tell Her Who Am I', often cracked Cooley up for hours on end.

The musicians with whom I engaged for this project are no strangers to quality dance music, fun and joviality. A good time was had with Ben Lennon and Peter Horan in Rosinver and with Johnny O'Leary at Dan Connell's in Knocknagree. Also, Peadar O'Loughlin, Vincent Broderick, Tommy Keane, Jacqueline McCarthy and Roger Sherlock unselfishly shared their time, hospitality and musical knowledge. And the ones who are gone must be remembered: Micho Russell and Joe Cooley.

An appreciation of traditional music can be gained from many fine sessions and concert performances or from listening to any of the numerous recordings available. The lives, curiosities, commentaries and personalities of the musicians and singers featured herein may offer further insight into the greater world of Irish traditional music.

I owe a debt of gratitude to many people for help with this book: Nicholas Carolan, Bernard Flaherty, Jackie Small, Dermot Healy, Muiris Ó Rócháin, Séamus Mac Mathúna and Dan O'Connell. Thanks also to Frances Marriott for the tune transcription and Frances L. Watt for use of her dissertation on Micho Russell.

CHARLIE PIGGOTT

Collecting the material for this book involved intruding into the private lives of people who are known to most of the music world only by rumour, reputation, stage performance and casual encounter. It opens a door on lives and experiences all so different as to make almost shocking the fact that its people have comfortably moved in and out of each other's experience since the 1930s. All have affected each other — either through the call of recorded music, or by their different styles and interpretation. Many have played together, some regularly, some momentarily. Others have shared the same spaces in time at *fleadhanna* or sessions without ever having met. Put together, they make not a blend but a mosaic of highly coloured differences in personality, self-image and world view.

The people in these pages see the music variously as habit, sheer pleasure, cultural artefact and artistic treasure. Their individual ways are the route-map of different pasts and presents in Irish music. Lucy Farr watches sets and listens to song at a keyhole in 1920s Ballinakill, Len Graham's father tunes to Athlone on his radio set up in Glenarm. Then there is the astonishment of the young Anthony MacMahon as he is struck by the spirituality of Cooley's angst drawn out of metal reeds on the instrument that almost consigned the uilleann pipes to the museum, and the young Néillidh Mulligan immersed in the swirl of piping and fiddles of his fathers' friends 'every one of whom turned out to have been a legend.' There is Pádraigín Ní Uallacháin's shock at unravelling the mystery of Mary Harvessy's song imprisoned for decades in manuscript; Mairéad Ní Mhaonaigh, Treasa Ní Cheannabháin and Maighread Ní Dhómhnaill for whom the archives were all alive. There is Brian Vallely committing Felix Doran to canvas, Paddy Keenan being asked to follow him to England, while Paddy Canny recalls his visits to east Clare. Brendan Begley is given an apple in Estonia, Liz Carroll receives a National Arts Endowment Award in Washington. Then we see Ann Mulqueen at fourteen with the only traditional song in the senior All-Ireland, and Róisín El-Saftay learning from her maternal 'master', Anne Conroy, on stage in Milan. Mary Bergin faces an audience of seven thousand in Denmark and Eithne Vallely transcribes tunes for Breathnach's *Ceol Rince na Éireann* in 1962.

Compiling this book has been intensely moving. It peels back layers of social change, degrees of poverty and technological erosion. Each story is conditioned by invisible political machinery: the obligation of emigration for Vincent Campbell and Séamus Ó Dubháin to toil 'deep in the heart of London town', while Joe Burke and Martin Hayes play for their ballrooms of romance. Decades later comes the confidence of Sharon Shannon in her home place. We hear Gary Hastings recollect the man from the Fermanagh Orange Hall letting go in what can only be *sean nós* dance, Sarah Anne O'Neill's father doing the same in 1920s Tyrone, Séamus Ó Dubháin bursting with the Connemara art on stage in modern New York.

It has been a privilege to explore and document these lives. It would not have been possible without the awesome tolerance of Evelyn Conlon. Nor could it have happened when it did without Niamh Parsons, who transformed the spoken word into print on Tom Sherlock's technology. My thanks, above all, to the people themselves for their patience with recollection, talking and proofing, for the hospitality, tolerance and understanding from them and their families, for all the sandwiches, cups of tea, bracing whiskeys, Christmas cake and mince pies that fuelled this endeavour through mid-winter.

FINTAN VALLELY

Summer 1969, a budding photographer full of youth and wonder, I arrived in Dublin on my first ever international assignment.

I soon met up with Galway man Joe Dolan.

Our usual meeting place was O'Donoghue's of Merrion Row . . .

. . . where Hughie McCormack, Frank Bryson, . . .

. . . Luke, John Kelly, Barney McKenna, Clive Collins . . .

. . . and Tommy . . . had a daily competition for seats in the back room where the best craic was.

Paddy kept a watchful eye on his drinking patrons. Himself and Maureen, his wife, were great supporters of the music and very kind to us all.

One Sunday morning early, they organised a welcome home party for Joe Heaney. He worked as a lift-man in the States and half of Connemara was waiting for him. A banner had been hung across the alley.

Joe had a face carved in granite and I had never heard
anyone singing like that.

The breakfast over, everyone sang for Joe. I took that picture of himself,
Seán Ó Conaire — alias 007 — and Tom Munnelly listening
to old Ted Furey singing.

Here is the King — long life to the King! Seamus Tansey posing for me in Strokestown House. Ask him for the tune and the story of 'The Wild Geese'.

Meet the street squad: 'the late' Mick O'Connor (alive, but always late),
banjo, Denis McMahon, fiddle (under the hat), John Caukley and gang.
Here at the All-Ireland fleadh in Listowel.

John Carty, a mighty banjo and fiddle player and, according to him, a bad fisherman. He lives near Boyle, County Roscommon, where I lived for many years.

Seán Lennon and Matt Cranitch in a back room in Milltown.
Seán is heavy on the bow, hence the picture.

Tomás Ó Nialláin and 'The Brown Man'. Here, at the county fleadh in Tulla,
Tomás is a great bodhrán player and 'The Brown Man' is a great set dancer.
Tomás is checking the dancer's hooves!

Seamus Cooley's Hooley

b.1929, d.1997

Seamus is dead. We all gathered to put him back where he came from – in the damp, rich, crumbly soil of south Galway. It is a wild 'end of the winter' day and we all shelter from the storm and the hailstones in a packed church.

Wizard box player Joe Burke is pulling tears out of my eyes as he plays 'The Wounded Huzzar' somewhere behind the pulpit. Grim faces, crying kids, incense, reels and jigs.

That big brown coffin in front of the altar.

Among the 'massy' things are a hurley and a tin whistle. The special blessed things: a man's life résumé.

Talk of birth, playing hurling and hammering notes out of various instruments, house-dances, *céilís*, crossroads, emigration.

Born in 1929, he did what they all did: emigrated to London in 1949, where he worked and played millions of tunes in the Irish pubs, the Irish clubs – and tunes in his head when digging tunnels and shovelling concrete.

On to Chicago with the Tulla Céilí Band . . . he stayed. Played and played, and played more: drinks, tunes, drinks, tunes, sleep, work, drinks, tunes, drinks, work, tunes, tunes, drinks, drinks, drinks . . . it is all a blur.

We've all trooped outside the church; Séamus's coffin is last.

The weather is vicious and it is a wet and miserable walk through a mucky lane to the graveyard. Muiris has a puncture. I am holding the umbrella on top of a shivering priest leading us into a hurried, mournful, ancient-like, soporific decade of the rosary. The wind blows my umbrella from my hand and I say, 'Oh, fuck.' His face, shining with raindrops, is full of reproach. 'Sorry, Father,' I mutter. The ones that heard laugh.

The coffin is down. It is pouring from the heavens.

Charlie and Peter take out their accordions and blast out a few reels. Brave old John Moloney, bent in two over his fiddle; his fingers are blue and his nose is dribbling with the cold. A few more tunes: 'Cooley's Reel', 'The Bucks of Oranmore'.

All of us drenched bucks, watched over broken hedges by bewildered sileage-munching bullocks, scatter back down the traffic-jammed lane. Now it is back in the pub for the real business of drinking tea, hot whiskeys, pints of Guinness, and wolfing down mounds of ham sandwiches. Young Timmy Tully's plate is full of uneaten crusts.

We all played and danced for two days.

Seamus is gone,
He is played out.

NUTAN

Seamus Cooley was buried on a blustery winter day after which Oliver Rowland,
Joe Burke, John Maloney and friends all gathered in Dooleys' of Peterswell
(where Seamus was born) for sandwiches, tea, drinks, tunes and set dances.

I remember sitting in a packed hall in Listowel for the finals of the céilí band competition. The atmosphere was electric. I was sitting with P. Joe Hayes and his wife Peggy. P. Joe is a real gentleman and Peggy, God bless her, bakes a mean rhubarb tart!

While fishing and living in Carrick, County Donegal, I always brought Con Cassidy and Mary Kate down to Teelin or Carrick of a Friday or Saturday night. There I met Dermot Byrnes, a genius box player in short trousers. Hidden behind glasses of Lucozade and a collection of cheese-and-onion Taytos, Dermot would play effortlessly in sessions with Con, James Byrne and the like. Many years later, when Dermot joined Altan, I met up with Ciarán Curran. The first thing Ben Lennon ever said to me in the streets of Milltown was: 'Have you seen young Curran?' Ben loves playing with him.

Brendan Begley

BY FINTAN VALLELY

I've seen the Atlantic, both wild and frantic
Swell those cliffs with an angry foam
Swing back defeated like knaves retreating
Through foam and fret from my Kerry home

FROM 'THE KERRY HILLS'

'That was my trip to Tír na nÓg. On one island we were the first strangers to be there in forty years. Some local musicians, they were following us around, and this fella came up to me one night, he says, "When ye play, ye bring the fairies back. The Russians killed all ours." I never got such a reaction to music. There were two thousand people one night in the open air and they were listening to just tunes. People were running up to us. One night a woman gave me an apple — it was probably all she had, like — and she said, "You haven't changed the course of Estonian history, but you've created a chapter." We were treated like — not rock stars — but as if we were from another planet!'

So Brendan Begley of Baile na mBoc, Ballyferriter, County Kerry, describes his music tour to Estonia just as things in the Warsaw-Pact countries began to open up in 1988. A long way, this, from playing for sets at home, or in Hughes's pub in Dublin where he energised set dancing for ten years.

Travel was in the genes, however, for back in the early century Brendan's grandfather Mickey Begley had a speakeasy in New York city, and a fish-curing shed, then a pub, at home in Ballydavid. Hard times and his passion for music converted the shed to a dance-hall when the curing finished. Brendan's mother, Mary Ellen Lynch, was a singer. Her own father had died with a song on his lips, and her maternal grandfather, Tommy Ferris, was a noted fiddler, the first of three generations of that name playing the instrument. Brendan's father sang, too, and played melodeon: 'I remember him playing in the dark on a summer's evening – you could see the sparks flying from his hobnail boots on the floor – and I'm not bullshitting when I say that,' Brendan recalls.

House parties were frequent, particularly in the summer months, with the annual flush of visiting 'Yanks'. As the youngest, Brendan first remembers these from the sounds filtering through to the bedroom. 'Singing was the main thing. You could hear anything – back to back there might be "South of the Border", "An Buachaill Caol Dubh" and "Sliabh na mBan". Even out milking the cows we might be singing.' His sister Jós recalls the 'ball nights' – the local emigrant 'wakes' – a few times a year, where sets would be danced too. But instrumentalists were thin enough on the ground in her childhood years of the 1950s.

All the Begleys would play or sing, and still do: Jós, James, Brendan, and Máire professionally. Their father's melodeon was always there, 'just in the house, like a computer might be today,' says Brendan. 'Everybody had a go at it.'

'Máire was mad for music before she could even walk,'

says Mary Ellen. 'She was playing from seven or eight and got a piano accordion at fourteen. And James [Séamus] was very interested always – he would go and learn a new tune and just come in and play it; we got him his own accordion at twelve or thirteen. In those years Josephine [Jós] was working very hard at the cows; it was only in later years that she had the time to play the concertina. Brendan was the youngest and he imitated James and Máire. But it was that [their father's] box that started them all off.'

The dance-hall at Muiríoch serviced a local demand – old time waltzes and quicksteps were the currency that left Jós with a particular love of dancing. 'But it was taken for granted that you knew the sets as well,' she says.

For Brendan, 'The dance-hall was a motivation to play. It had all the céilí dances, but you'd find the sets in the pub.' The céilí dances had started with the Irish colleges in the 1950s, and in 1955 the hall was done up properly as a 'ballroom of romance' dance-hall, finally closing in 1980.

'There were no pipes around the place, and no fiddles either,' says Brendan of his younger years and the dance-hall scene. 'I saw a neighbour play a fiddle once – but here it was all dance music and the fiddle couldn't be heard. The accordion was the loudest instrument, and the music was for dancing – full stop – so it took over. They'd listen to airs OK, but music was for dancing.'

The dancers were fussy, too, and what prevailed in the rest of the country had no home here. 'I remember, when I started playing reels, they'd actually come up to me and say they hated reels. They danced to jigs, hornpipes, polkas and slides.' This is how sets were danced locally when they first arrived there more than a century ago. Cost, of course, was a big factor in how music was made too; there was just no spare cash: 'Melodeons were very cheap to buy in comparison to fiddles. They reckon that four or five fellas would put together and they'd buy a melodeon and they'd go out on the Wran then. So they must have been cheap.'

Sessions were different then. Music was for dancing to, not playing for pleasure. If one player could do the job, then why have more? 'If you were asked to play in a pub, you'd play a couple of tunes and they'd listen, next thing they'd dance sets, next thing they'd start singing and then you'd play a few more tunes. That was the session, you know; you had the three together.'

This was important to the notion of 'style' in playing. There was no standardisation: 'There were nine or ten musicians around the place, but I never saw them playing together – they all played separately. And, as a result, they all had their own different styles. OK, they had the swing and the wildness, but they each had a unique style.'

At the age of twenty, in 1973, Brendan went to the National College of Physical Education in Limerick, now University College Limerick. 'That was the biggest change in my life ever. I remember being inside in the digs, and the woman of the house called me and it was the first time I was ever called in English. It was literally like landing in France or China. I could understand English, but I couldn't really converse easily. And then going into PE – that was a new thing! And at least 70% of the teachers were English, and they all had English accents. I'd say that was the biggest culture shock that I ever got, having done all my education through Irish and then be landed with lecturers who didn't even have an Irish accent.' And there was another contradiction too. For at home and school he had never played any sports. 'I went to a PE college and I'd never played football! I think I togged out the first time ever at the age of 18!' But he had rowed curraghs in the Dingle regatta, and went on to play rugby for the college and for the Dingle team.

Moving to Dublin in 1977 to teach in Coláiste Mhuire brought him to a social scene where there were more shocks in store: 'When I went to Dublin I found it difficult to sit down and just play tunes all night, and then go to the *góilín* (singers' club) and sing all night, and then go to the Pipers' Club – and they danced all night! It was just like when the mixed farming went out of vogue, like; it was all specialised!'

However, he adjusted, and played in Club a' Chonraidh in Harcourt Street first. Then when he moved out to Lucan they had sessions in the Spa Hotel until 1984. A request from set dance teacher Terry Moylan got him out of there playing for Pipers' Club sets – *céilíthe* – at the Ormond Hotel. Then they had a session in the Bark Kitchen, and finally, 'my brother-in-law asked me would I play in his sister's place, so we started in Hughes's in September 1985'.

On that first night Brendan played with Cork fiddler Gerry Bevin, guitarist Steve Cooney and whistle player Vinnie Kilduff: 'There were only seven or eight in the place – they just barely had enough for a half set!' He played in Lucan then with Larry Kinsella (concertina) and Patsy Toland (banjo) from Donegal, with Tulla concertina player Mary McNamara, and ex-pupil Paul McGrattan, and had 'rakes of music with Dermot McLoughlin [fiddler]. I found that the Donegal style of music has the same wildness as Kerry. The only difference was the tempo. I mean, it didn't have the hump in it – not the steady kind of hump that you do for dancing.'

But the metropolis never agreed with Brendan. A persistent serious throat infection frighteningly drained him of energy. Medical science had no answers, and then acupuncturist Ronnie Turner changed his diet and 'told me to just get out of the city, it's getting to you'. Back in Tralee teaching in 1995, things were no better, so he 'just packed it in and decided to go at music full-time'. As luck would have it, the very next day he was telephoned and asked to take piper Christy O'Leary's empty chair in the Boys of the Lough. He also has his own group, Beginish. His solo album, *We Won't Come Home Till Morning*, is his matchless testimonial, but he has sessioned too on Chieftains albums and for the Boys of the Lough.

His children play different instruments – concertina, fiddle, accordion. 'They're kind of laying off it now, but they'll come back to it. I probably taught them not to play!

I was just too intense myself. So I said, "Fuck it! No more!" I was getting too cross. I'd love to see them play music, because it opens so many doors to you. But the most important thing would be that I could be friends with them.'

Music remains his 'only acceptable form of madness. This is my second language now, without boundaries. It's like being in the open sea: you can turn any way you want and go anywhere you want – that's when you're feeling good about it. It's completely without rules within itself and it's the time when I have the most freedom to do what I really want to do. You can't eat it or drink it or jump on top of it, but for me it's totally innovative within itself. If I play a tune I learned from somebody else, I never play it like anybody else. When I'm going wild at it, I'm just there beside it!' He feels that the Bill Whelans and Mícheál Ó Súilleabháins of this world present traditional music to new audiences: 'To me, Horslips attracted so many people, too, and they have never been credited with it. They mightn't have meant anything for the traditional musicians, but people got introduced. And then they might have thought that they had it all, so then they'd try again – better, look further. And then they'd go to the roots.'

Music, in his childhood, was never recognised as a career or a good thing to be doing. A musician was always seen as a person that 'couldn't go out and do a hard day's work – just a bit of a fool. But now he'd be respected. There's way more respect for music and musicians now because it is being recognised outside of Ireland. In Dingle, when the tourists came in looking for traditional music, the pubs all jumped on the bandwagon. And now people's "ears" are getting better.'

Brendan has always learned mostly from fiddle players: 'If I had my way, I'd prefer to play the fiddle!' All the Begleys grew up being told 'When you are big you'll be playing for the *céilís* in the hall,' and Brendan's first gig was at the age of twelve when he was told 'You're playing the drums tonight.' The nine years he spent doing just that while working at the accordion taught him rhythm, and today he is a superb player for dancing.

His sister, Máire, has stories of a priest in the 1930s who used to stand outside the Begley Hall at Muiríoch demanding its closure. She relates the drama of another who regularly 'read it out' from the pulpit with the chilling epithet: 'The devil is below in the hall!' Later, in the 1950s when the local curate built his own hall with parish money, it was remarked to him, 'I see you have shifted the divil over.' Back where he belongs, in Ballydavid, the divil that is music has Brendan where he wants him.

Beir mo dhúthracht go dúthaigh Duibhneach
('Send my devotion to Corca Dhuibhne')

FROM THE POEM BY AN SEABHACH SHUGRUE

Mary Bergin

BY FINTAN VALLELY

Mary Bergin is one of the younger Dublin city people who, in the 1960s, began dispersing the illusion that traditional music's natural domain is the deep country. There were few musicians around, few sessions, little technology and not much transport. In 1968 she won the All-Ireland senior tin whistle championship and, over the following five years, became known as an inveterate session player.

In 1979 she made an outstanding and unequalled album of whistle music — *Feadóg Stáin*. That first record says as much about her as her own words. Gushing with baroque ornament yet uncluttered, a bubbling cheekiness without trying superiority, crisp articulation, intense and focused emotion, her playing is honestly direct. She is one of those who came of age in the revival of traditional music and upon whom its present has been built. Mary's mother, both a traditional and a trained fiddler herself, had grown up in a family of classically oriented musicians in County Wicklow. Her father, with no music in his own Kilkenny family, played melodeon.

Mary Bergin was born in 1949 in Shankhill, County Dublin, at a time when it was still country and trees and a trip to Dublin was a yearly outing. Music was an important part of her younger life — her mother stopping playing after her brother Seán was born. But her parents did have interest in and associations with music. She was sent to learn piano, but only remembers the teacher always saying rosaries. She picked up the whistle at about the age of nine, getting hooked on it after hearing Willie Clancy play at an Oireachtas concert in Dublin. No one else around her was playing. Her father was her only early influence – they played together after mass on a Sunday. And, oddly enough for those years, radio – and its influential *Ceolta Tíre* and *Job of Journeywork* programmes – played no conscious part in Mary's musical beginnings. 'We had no radio and we listened to no records.' But people were invited in: 'Mrs Harrington [fiddler, and sister of the Sligo flute player John Joe Gardiner] and Mrs Crotty [the Clare concertina player] called once. That was a memorable night for me. It got me going out to local sessions.'

She began going to *fleadhanna* in the 1960s, and to sessions in Blackrock with fiddlers Joe Liddy and Seán O'Dwyer, and blind whistle player Terry Horan. This was the foundation of a repertoire. Her territory expanded with age, leading her to meet other players in Dublin at the Claremen's Club in Church Street and the Thomas Street Pipers' Club sessions.

She entered tin whistle competitions from the age of fourteen, then she took up the flute at the age of sixteen or so. When someone fell on it at a session, though, she abandoned it until recently. 'Competition in the past was different – we all knew each other, we would all play together. I knew Peg McGrath [flute player from Roscommon, killed tragically in 1993] well. We might be playing in the jacks, and then going in competing with each other! It didn't mean anything.'

Fleadhanna are not memorable for her; she stopped going when she won the All-Ireland. 'I was always in bits. I like playing with people I know, even if I do enjoy meeting new people. My favourite place is a session in the back room of a pub.' At Sion Hill school in Blackrock, and in common with many at that time, she found attitudes debilitating: 'Mary and her tin whistle – tiddly-diddly, they would say. Contempt.' She worked for Radio Éireann in Henry Street, Dublin, then was head-hunted for Comhaltas's headquarters in Monkstown: 'I had done a library course, and a broadcasting and recording course. My interest was in working with music and musicians. I was told I would be working in the library, but they asked me to do the accounts instead!'

When she married Australian flute-maker Bruce De Ve in 1978 she moved to County Galway to work at their instrument business, to play and teach. Living now in Spiddal for the last twenty years, she has come through tough times with travelling, and playing and teaching music.

Music is a passion, she feels, and Galway is a place where people can give themselves to it in the same way as her generation did in the 1960s and 1970s: 'It's there in every doorway. It's fantastic. I think music is communication – there to be shared. It's a gas – I can see the young musicians playing music non-stop as I would have done myself. It just takes up their whole lives. When I stand back and take a look at it, it's a kind of madness in itself. It's amazing to see it the second time around!'

Her own two children – 16 and 15 – are living on the edge of all this, being just themselves and their age. Mary would like them to get involved, but she doesn't believe in forcing them or making decisions for them. 'They play, and I'm guiding them to get enthusiastic about playing tunes. We've got a group of maybe twenty-five teenagers here – all of them playing – and we're trying to get them geared into having a session, as a social thing. I say to myself, "Jesus, do I really want them to get so totally focused on their music?" Ah, but I do! I think, in the long run, it's a healthy thing. There are an awful lot worse things they could be doing than music.' Galway, of course, has all the problems of any growing city, and Mary sees sections which are disadvantaged, and children without hope or direction. For her own, she can at least point them in a direction in which they won't be bored.

Teaching music presents problems. Mary feels that a lot of kids will get just so far, and then, at the point when they could be encouraged to go the magic bit further, there are no facilities. Too young for the pub, too old for just classes. 'There are sessions in the pubs here, but a lot of the parents don't particularly want to be guiding their kids there for the moment. What is really needed is that music should become a social thing among the children. They should want to play and to go places.' She and some friends have organised a Sunday morning session just for them, 'to try to keep them young for as long as they are, rather than throwing them into the adult music world too early. What

we do helps them to get to know each other as a group. It will extend into something else, but for now I'm happy that they're able to play a few tunes.'

A lot of children in the area are learning at the moment. Some travel the fifteen miles to Galway for tuition from well-known names. Locally, most learn the whistle first. 'Strange, really, because this is accordion country. Whistles and fiddles were alien instruments here!' Mary does in fact encourage some of her pupils to take up the box or concertina. She teaches both locally and in Galway city, but her reputation is good and some pupils travel long journeys to her – from Moycullen, the islands and Rossaveel. She teaches in schools, too, during normal hours, under the auspices of Ceol Acadamh, run by Údarás na Gaeltachta. She teaches by standard, not age, as this is fairer to all. 'When I came here first from teaching kids in Dublin I could get nowhere, because they literally had had no exposure to music before. Now I start them on singing the scale.' Interest is so great that Mary believes the only restriction is the lack of suitable music teachers.

Mary Bergin is known all over the island as a solo player. Many of her spots she does with bouzouki player Alec Finn of De Danann, but she has slid into the comfort of group playing with her own Dordán in recent years. 'It's so much easier travelling in company. It can be lonely travelling places just on your own. Whereas, if you're with the others, there's company and a bit of *craic*, even if there's less money.' Dordán's mix of O'Carolan and baroque music places them in a market not open to others – 'corporate gigs', after dinners, 'and sometimes we perform through a dinner, which can be really demoralising'.

She feels that too many people today use accompaniment as a kind of crutch. 'The solo instrument isn't often heard any more. I'd like to get back to solo performance again, even though it's much more difficult because you're so vulnerable on your own. But people enjoy it and will pay attention.' Coming to baroque music was strange for her: 'I'm not great at reading a piece of music – I'm much better at picking it up by ear. My playing of baroque pieces would be in a traditional style because I have no classical training. So we would usually pick a piece with a strong melody line. I tried to do the actual ornamentation that was written down on just one piece – and that was interesting, for the ornamentation was nearly the reverse of what I would do normally.'

Working herself in 'passing on' music in schools, she is pleased that her son Colm chose to do his Junior Cert music through traditional performance: 'I didn't force him. He picked it himself because it's becoming more popular now.' But she feels that the content of music in the schools is being weakened and that a lot of the examiners have no knowledge of traditional music: 'There should be discussion about it. If there's going to be traditional music in education let it be done in an authentic way. Traditional musicians should be doing the examination – there are enough people able to do it. And there should be a broad panel from around the country, because there are different styles and attitudes.'

For most of her group, Dordán, travel is limited by the demands of rearing children, so they are selective about what they do. Group playing makes different demands from solo playing. Dordán has a light, melody-rich sound and this can cause problems: 'One festival organiser told us that we wouldn't be "suitable" for festivals, that we hadn't got "the sound that the audiences want". They said that kids abroad needed to hear that big, heavy sound of guitars, that they go for rhythm, and tunes mean nothing to them; they wouldn't know a jig from a reel. But, in actual fact, in festivals abroad we get a great response. Given the choice, the audiences *do* appreciate how different our music is. And, for that matter, the loud stuff can just as easily "all sound the same" too, and be quite boring!'

Mary Bergin sees herself as a soloist in the older repertoire of traditional music. She believes in the importance of regional differences and styles of playing. 'I don't like to see Riverdance and all of this being classified as "traditional" music. It's Irish music, it's coming out of Ireland, but it is not *traditional* music and it is being confused all the time with it. I think a lot of the new-age Irish music is not Irish traditional music. The conformity, the patterns, have altered and I think it's taken away from it.'

Like most players, she finds it hard to define, in words, a 'traditional' tune – but knows one when she hears one. She has written pieces herself to fit Dordán's arrangements, and full tunes too, only she finds she has not the time to sit down to it. Both her 1979 album and her 1989 one are entitled *Feadóg Stáin* (literally, 'tin whistle'), indicating her confidence in the music she plays, free of any other images. She listens to a lot of *sean nós* song, and is pleased that musicians have moved away from wall-to-wall reels towards jigs, hornpipes, barndances, airs. She feels that these days there is more emphasis on the technical rather than the rhythmic. 'Stockton's Wing and Moving Hearts did nothing for me,' she says. 'De Danann I like. They play fast but lose nothing. They're tight.' Frankie Gavin and Cork flute player Conall Ó Gráda have the style Mary Bergin admires —

'uplifting' — it is the subtle difference that sets out the particular player. 'Tommy Peoples is one of the saddest musicians I have experienced. I have cried listening to him play. It's like that — one version of a tune can make my night.'

Joe Burke
and
Anne Conroy

BY FINTAN VALLELY

My father played the melodeon
Outside at our gate
There were stars in the morning east
And they danced to his music.

FROM 'A CHRISTMAS CHILDHOOD' BY PATRICK KAVANAGH

Joe Burke and Anne Conroy are two of traditional music's most gentle souls and calm, passionate musicians. Theirs is the music of place – jigs and reels invested with the energy of post-famine reconstruction and new-society identification. Joe's musicianship and early professionalism now accord him 'living legend' status here and in America, a grand old – but still young – man of the music. He learned to play in the climate of De Valera's new Republic. The musicians of his teenage years ooze the frantic discovery of past artistic grandeur, and burst with dignity in awareness of local style. Players of Joe's era and stature are usually found in America, where the music was maintained in service to Irish exiles as an important part of community identity. Distanced by a generation, Anne's route has overlapped in music-making with the personalities of Joe's childhood, her musicianship propelling her off the 'revival' springboard into the new-interest centres of Ireland and Europe.

Joe was born at Coorhoor, above Loughrea in County Galway, in 1939. His mother came from a family of musicians just three miles away at Ballinagrieve. She played melodeon, her brother, Paddy Kane, played flute and Clarke's whistle. She and Joe's uncle, Pat Burke, used to play melodeons for the house-dances, that continued up to the 1950s. Joe's father and grandfather played the flute too. Although uncertain of the number of aunts and uncles, Joe is sure of ages and pedigree: 'My last aunt over in Omaha, Nebraska, left Ireland in 1917. She lived to be 99. And she played a melodeon that she got from the grocer's shop for coupons in 1912.'

While young people in town would be talking about 'jazz', 'out here we played hurling and danced sets. In Loughrea, the Town Hall had a beautiful floor, but they wouldn't allow any Irish dances because hobnail boots were not good for the maple.' Hall *céilí* dances overlapped with the end of the house-dances that were still held right up to the late 1950s: at Christmas, before Lent, for people back on summer holidays, for thrashings and 'stations'. 'They'd play cards, too, and on those nights they'd dance sets in the kitchen. I used to play for sets with melodeons, fiddle players and flute players at those, and at Christmas time there would be mummers' spree!' Musicians were plentiful, and they'd play in pairs for a stretch of an hour. Others were playing in *céilí* bands. All were respected locally. 'On a Monday morning people would be talking about where they were the night before, what musicians, what *céilí* band, and who was with the band – a great consciousness.' In east Galway there were no fewer than sixteen bands, with seven or eight players in each. Some were famous. Indeed, the

Ballinakill were the first to broadcast on Radio Éireann, then came the Aughrim Slopes in 1932.

This was 1954, the beginning too of music played for the pleasure of it. Sessions were arranged during the week in certain local houses – particularly in Aggie White's, Downey and Paddy Fahy's Killabeg house. These were fiddlers – Downey and Fahy were also composers – but accordion players Kevin Keegan and Joe Cooley were sought-after company too: 'Fahy would keep you all night. Just when you'd be leaving, he'd take out the fiddle to play you the latest tune he'd composed and then it would be daylight!' Knowledgeable about electrics, Fahy's famous prank was rigging a microphone upstairs to the radio downstairs: 'They'd be all talking around the fire and he'd go upstairs and play into it. "Oh Jesus, that's Fahy! He's playing on the radio again tonight!"'

When he was growing up, there was always a gramophone in the Burke house. Joe's earliest memory is of Meath accordionist Michael Grogan's 78s. Joe began playing at the age of four. He remembers fiddler Martin Hanny on a settle bed at a 'station' (house mass) playing 'The Swallow's Tail'. 'I remember thinking: if I could only get that sound on the accordion!' Joe was 'mad into it'; farmwork was all set music. 'Oh Jesus! There was nothing to talk about only the music and I used be around here and I'd think of nothing else!' he says of his teenage years.

For that age group, the *fleadh cheoil* was the inspiring movement. Joe's first was in Loughrea in 1955, where he came third in the under-18 accordion. Next year he was pipped by Tony MacMahon (but won seniors in 1959 and 1960). They would play together in Ennis with accordionist Raymond Roland, who was home on holidays with a rented car. 'When the money ran out he would go back to Leeds.' Joe eventually played with Raymond's brother Oliver in the Leitrim (parish) Céilí Band, which had begun in Downey's house. Through the late 1950s Joe played with the band in all the famous meccas of the dancing Irish in London – the Gresham Ballroom and the Round Tower on Holloway Road, the Galtymore in Cricklewood, Gloccamara in Bayswater, the Blarney on Tottenham Court Road, the Garryowen in Hammersmith, the Hibernian in Fulham Broadway, the Harp Club in New Cross. 'There were thousands of people dancing in the halls – "Siege of Ennis", "Stack of Barley", old-time waltzes, sets – ah, it was great, it was mighty.'

Joe's reputation was growing, and a meeting with Seán Ó Síocháin (of the GAA) at the Swinford *fleadh* of 1961 led to a tour of America with him, Gráinne McCormack (dancer, married to Martin Fay of the Chieftains), and Kathleen Watkins (harpist, married to Gay Byrne). Fifteen cities in two weeks – all organised by letter – New York, Chicago, Boston, Detroit, Atlanta. Furthest west was Greely, Nebraska. 'The great plains of Nebraska, for me coming from a farm, I couldn't believe it. And didn't I meet cowboys! And the Governor's wife. It was covered on the front pages of the Omaha press. Jesus Christ, it's beyond belief now! To be able to come home and say, "I was in Nebraska", and show them the papers – full pages. Of all the trips I've done since then, none was as exciting for any reason as that.'

Bill Fuller got Joe to stay on for a weekend to play at his City Centre Ballroom in New York. There he met the piano player Felix Dolan and fiddler Paddy Killoran. Fuller invited Joe back, offering him gigs in his New York, Chicago and Boston halls. 'I came home here and looked around and it seemed an awful good offer then. So I took off!' It all seemed so simple. They dressed formally. They played an old-time waltz, the 'Stack of Barley' and the 'Siege of Ennis', this in three fifteen-minute spots between the Fintan Ward Band's sets. The accompaniment was piano and drums. They played Fuller's halls in rotation – a city a week – and the money was good: 'I used to get a great kick out of it. More money than the bus drivers! For my couple of tunes!' But the travel and routine became tiresome, and hard work too. Joe wanted time to associate with the great American fiddlers, Andy McGann, Larry Redican, Jack Coen and Paddy Reynolds. Offers of Gaelic League *céilíthe* and such lured him away and eventually he came back to Ireland 'for good', playing solo, trading on a reputation made from Irish airplay of a 1965 tribute to Michael Coleman record he'd made with Andy McGann and Felix Dolan.

During his absence, the Dubliners had started. Traditional music was becoming popular, and commercial too. Bill Fuller had taken note, and had Joe play at the opening night of his Teach Furbó in Barna, Galway, then in his Old Sheiling at Raheny, Dublin. Bar concerts were scarce, but Joe's first was with Seán Maguire (fiddle) at The Rustic Inn in Abbeyshrule, Longford. This led to a recording with Maguire and Josephine Keegan, and six years of playing together – folk clubs in Scotland and England, and all over Ireland. He began touring for Comhaltas in the US in 1972, and he continued to travel back and forwards there himself. He began recording his own albums as 'Shaskeen' after 1965.

All her life Anne Conroy had been almost a neighbour of Joe. Born in 1959 at Wellpark, Abbey, the confidence of the music revival was all around. Her father Bernie, a farmer and carpenter who worked by day in Tynagh Mines, played fiddle and had a *céilí* band. 'Every parish had its *céilí* band, but this one was nearly all Conroys. Some were related, some not so. I was always mad to take off and go along to wherever my father was going,' says Anne. Bernie's own mother – Mary Kate Fahy – had a reputation as a melodeon and concertina player for the house-dances of her day. She had a large family, and Bernie's elder sister in England used to send back money to pay for his fiddle lessons with a woman in Portumna. His brother Connie also played accordion, and they all sang. Anne's mother had no music, but as a child Anne experienced house-dancing on card nights and such. As a child she would work tunes on a cousin's accordion, getting her own when she was eight or nine.

Seven years younger than her sister, Anne spent a lot of time with her father. 'Do you know, he was great, when I think back on it! At the drop of a hat he would take me – when I was old enough – anywhere there was a session. He introduced me to a lot of musicians. I would have been fairly close to him.' Music had moved out of people's houses by then, so Bernie brought Anne to pub sessions. Among these, Moylan's of Loughrea, with flute player Paddy Carty, was famous in the early 1970s. Lucy Farr and many other music exiles were continually passing through. Carty was always a focus for great music, as were other 'regulars' – Paddy Fahy, John Joe Forde (accordion), Peter Broderick (flute), Seán Ac Donncha the *sean nós* singer who lived in Ahascragh. When Carty died, the session died too.

Anne began making forays into Dublin in 1980. She would spend weekends there taking part in the thrilling session life of those years, in Slattery's and the Four Seasons of Capel Street, the Béal Bocht in Portobello, the Man of Arran and the Brazen Head. 'Finbar Boyle [of the Tradition Club] was the first person to ask me to play professionally.' She joined singer Geraldine McGowan in the band Oisín and for seven years toured all over Europe. 'I kicked off in northern Italy. We had such a mighty time altogether, I nearly ended up living there.' This, and working for a travel agent, gave her itchy feet, and after a summer at the Willie Clancy week in Milltown Malbay, County Clare, she decided she wanted to make a living out of music. 'It was kind of a big step, because there wasn't too many women doing it — if there were any. It was mostly old men that I was hanging around with!'

Anne and Joe got married in 1990. A famous and respected duet, they play together on a circuit of festivals and familiar places in Ireland and the US. But the world of traditional music is changing, and since the 1960s there are now four or five generational groupings on the scene, almost independent of each other, and each progressively bigger than the earlier one. 'I go around at the Willie Clancy week, the Joe Cooley week, the Paddy O'Brien week — the Tobercurry week — and the *fleadh cheoil* week,' says Joe, 'and I don't hear any different from what you would hear fifty years ago. There is probably a better standard of players — and better instruments. But — Jesus Christ — there was a panic about where the traditional music was going, a few years ago!' Messing with the sacrosanct, however — especially in the context of east Galway — draws wit and fire from Joe: 'I get convulsions and sick when I hear some people's contortions. It can be so phoney and contrived, and so devoid of any consideration of music as far as I'm concerned. I just can't stand the way — the vandalism of the way — I've heard some of Paddy Fahy's music butchered!'

And Joe is a gentleman. There is no way of knowing how much the obligation of handing over the baton to an eager younger coterie affects the mature musician. Nor is there any way of telling how much a player's empathy with composer, style, region and place overshadows their potential appreciation of the new enthusiasm and talent which they dearly would like to welcome. Joe Burke and Anne Conroy are proud of the music they have inherited and play, and are passionate about the countryside they live in. Loughrea is no longer a centre of music. An older generation rest on their laurels, immersed in links with the past that are provocatively etched in the names of small townlands: Coorhoor, Coorheen, Coscorrig, Sonnagh, Ballinagrieve, Gorteenanillaun, Grallagh, Grousehill. And Kilnadeema, where the Burke–Conroy house is the living mausoleum of music-memory for all the stages of traditional music revival.

Vincent Broderick

BY CHARLIE PIGGOTT

The countryside north of Loughrea in County Galway is home to an interesting antiquity called the Turoe Stone. This famous, ornately decorated Iron Age monument sits only a stone's throw from Bullaun, where brothers Peter and Vincent Broderick were born and musically reared. Their grandmother was a cousin of the renowned Galway piper, Patsy Tuohey, and their mother Ann (a whistle player, born blind but cured at a holy well at the age of three) provided the indigenous musical environment for the brothers, close to the edge of Carramore bog under the sweeping gaze of the Sliabh Aughty mountains to the south. She possessed 'an awful ear for music. She had all the tunes and all the music you could think of that time.' Concert flutes bequeathed by a local parish priest were their instruments of choice and, by the time they reached teenage years, music making was second nature to them.

During the early and middle years of this century, south Galway was, in Vincent's words, 'alive with music'. It was everywhere. Jigs and reels could be heard resounding along lines running from Derrybrien through Ballinakill, Abbey and Killimor, and from Peterswell through Loughrea, Kilreekill and Aughrim.

Emerging from this musical landscape at the dawn of the *céilí*-band era were the legendary Old Ballinakill and the Aughrim Slopes. Musical families like the Fahys, Traceys, Maloneys and Brodericks contributed unselfishly to this tradition, where flute, fiddle and accordion dominate. Reel playing in this countryside is a science unto itself and the practice of musical composition is strong. The intricate, innovative and often complex outpourings of fiddle players Paddy Fahy and Paddy Kelly come to mind, and the inspiration for other compositions like those of Paddy O'Brien and Seán Ryan was not unconnected with south Galway music.

The greater part of Vincent Broderick's life and music has been devoted to composition. At first glance, the tune titles of his extensive collection (called *The Turoe Stone*) portray an impression of an understudy of natural history: 'The Fox on the Prowl', 'The Spider's Web', 'The Enchanted Lake'. There is also 'The Flagstone of Memories' — on whose time-worn surface last farewells were exchanged and the tearful steps of departing emigrants were heard outside cabin doors — and 'The Coachman's Whip', 'The Goat's Path' and 'The Cockstep in the Dunghill' — the distance covered by the stately cock's cautious, advancing, military-like step across the dung heap signifying the incremental increase in daylength from Small Christmas onwards.

Allusions to nature in traditional music come as no surprise. Many of the musicians of preceding generations were of a mountainy disposition. Their music is, at its core, elemental, surfacing as an expression of the vibrations and rhythms of the natural world — mountain streams, unseen spirits, birds and mammals — and the toils, tribulations and nuances of speech that are part and parcel of everyday country life.

Vincent vividly remembers — when domestic duties allowed — passing time leaning over the half-door beside his mother, who absorbed and understood the songs and flight-sounds of the birds: 'the jack-snipe and all the birds that would pass by and the wild geese at night-time. She could imitate every one of them.' He and his brothers grew up in this enchanting environment.

Carramore bog was their playground. On dreary, rain-filled days the house often buzzed with life and music — turf-cutters, neighbouring musicians, itinerant traders, or passers-by in need of shelter. One of Vincent's air compositions possesses the unusual title 'The Lighthouse in the Bog'. 'We lived on the side of the bog, you know, and at night-time there was always a light in the window. The mother would be up and you could see it from the main road. If there was a light in Broderick's house, it was still not too late. And my father used to go out hunting at five o'clock in the morning with a pair of greyhounds. He was getting old at the time, so he'd go to bed at six o'clock in the evening. And maybe at nine or ten o'clock, the lads would come in and the music would start up. And my father would waken up and he'd say: "Annie, what the hell kind of house are you keeping at all? This house is like a bloody lighthouse. There's a light every night of the week here, all night long." So we called it the Lighthouse in the Bog.'

Early 78 discs of the Old Ballinakill Band testify to the

fact that they played some of the finest Irish traditional music ever recorded, and the young Brodericks always felt honoured to have associated with these legendary musicians. 'There was a concert in Bullaun and the priest that was there had come down from the Ballinakill side. He knew the Ballinakill Band, which was playing that night for a *céilí* after the concert. And he knew, you see, that Peter and I loved the music and he asked the two of us to stay over after the concert to listen to the band. He told Tommie Whelan [the renowned flute player], who brought up the two of us to play for half an hour. I was twelve years of age that time.'

There is a tune in the tradition called 'Broderick's Reel', often referred to as 'Peter Broderick's', who must have played it countless times. It is, however, one of Vincent's compositions, with the given title 'The Tinker's Daughter'. The older brother also composed, but to a lesser extent, and one of Peter's tunes, 'The Thatcher's Mallet', has earned him a place in the annals: in 1954 he caused a sensation by entering Loughrea during the All-Ireland *fleadh cheoil* in possession of a home-made copper flute. He played 'The Thatcher's Mallet' that weekend and, to my knowledge, was the only individual ever to win an All-Ireland title playing a self-composed melody on a self-made instrument!

Besides his preoccupation with music, Vincent is also a storyman, a teller of tales. Embedded beneath the surface of his richly poetic tune titles lie connections, segments of life experiences waiting to be expressed. Clothed in story, the melodies seem to take on a greater life force. 'The Fox on the Prowl' is a fine reel, well entrenched in the tradition and played at many a music session.

Well, we were building houses outside Ballinasloe and at night-time we stayed in an old makeshift hut. And we used to go down card playing, across the field to a farmer's house. He had a lovely girl of a daughter and he didn't want her to be out at night with any lads or anything. So, when we'd start playing cards at ten or eleven o'clock at night, the farmer didn't know, but the mother knew well the girl had a boyfriend. And he'd come and he would rattle the henhouse door and the hens would all start cackling. And she'd say, 'Mary, go on out. That fox is on the prowl again tonight.' So that's how it got the name 'The Fox on the Prowl'.

The title of another of Vincent's reels, 'The Old Woman in the Glen', refers to the practice of *cuairtíocht* or visiting. Though once widespread throughout the Irish countryside, the recent abrupt decline of this tradition sadly reflects our changing lifestyles. Vincent relates that, some fifty years ago:

We were coming back from a Christmas mumming trip. We were finishing up about twelve o'clock. And I said, if we see one more light we'll go in. There might be some poor ol' divil in want of a visit, you know. So we were coming up around Abbey-knockmoy and we saw this light, in a field. So we went in a long boreen and there was a dog barking and a woman stuck her head out over a half-door and she said, 'Do ye know, I'm here since daybreak this morning and not a sinner ever called to the house. My husband is two months dead and I couldn't sit down to my dinner without somebody. Will ye eat the Christmas dinner with me?' So I said, 'Begod we will.' And I looked along the mantelpiece and there was fourteen photographs and they were all in America. The last one had gone in the June previous. And we stayed there and had the dinner with her. The old woman in the glen. I thought about it after and didn't we read in the paper where this woman was found dead inside a door. And 'twas the woman. We were probably the last ones that saw her alive. That's the memory I have of the Old Woman in the Glen.

The experiences portrayed through Vincent Broderick's music come from a rich and varied life. South-east Galway of the 1930s and 1940s held some ingrained memories: weddings, *céilíthe*, mumming activities and house-dances, where the bicycle was the transport of the day. 'Weddings were great,' he says, 'especially during the war. There was no food but there was plenty of drink and a meal for the musicians, whatever would happen.'

Many fine Sligo tunes were introduced to south Galway through the now legendary house-sessions at Roland's of Ballyshea, where the Broderick brothers exchanged music with Paddy Carthy, Mrs Harrington, Joe Leary and Joe Cooley. By all accounts, the music, dancing and *craic* were mighty. 'Old Paddy Meenahan was the god of them all, because he was a man who wanted no sound, only the sound of music.' On one occasion, a fiddle player was having difficulty bringing out the well-known reel, 'The Woman of the House', when Paddy, holding court, was heard to announce: 'That's not "The Woman of the House" I know.' Joe Cooley, who was present, instantly interjected with the comment: 'Ah, sure, there could be two women in that house,' gently diffusing the situation.

Vincent Broderick moved to Dublin in the early 1950s, associating himself with the Pipers' Club, Comhaltas Ceoltóirí Éireann, *céilí* bands, *scoraíochts* and broadcasting, while teaching whistle and flute. His family have inherited his music and he still composes whenever inspiration beckons.

The Mountain Stream

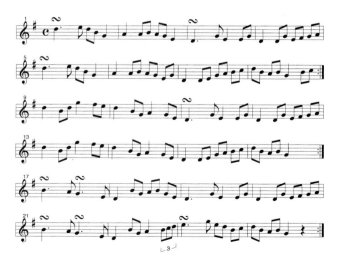

Regarding a recent composition, a barn-dance called 'The Mountain Stream', he has this to say:

I'll play this piece for you now. I'll give you a description of how I compose. So this piece is called 'The Mountain Stream' and I spend a lot of time up around the Dublin mountains. But where the Liffey rises near Sally's Gap, it flows under an iron bridge on the way to Blessington and it's just beginning to turn from a stream to a river. If you sit on that bridge of an evening, you can hear the water going through the rocks and there's a sound now like this . . . And one evening I was sitting there and I was listening to the wind whistling through the heather and an odd bird flying around and I thought I could form a tune from it. So this is the way it goes. You can get in the sound of the water and the birds. That's the way, usually. That's the way.

Vincent Campbell

BY FINTAN VALLELY

Vincent Campbell and his brother Jimmy are among the great musicians of County Donegal. They have an easy, authoritative and intelligent confidence in the mixed repertoire they have inherited. A native speaker of Irish, Vincent talks passionately about 'the big glen' where they were born, where their ancestors too farmed and fiddled for generations among the bleak beauty of the Croaghs (Blue Stack Mountains), an area now rendered silent by emigration and migration.

Their present gentle joy in their art masks other lives lived, things seen and hardships endured. For both Campbells worked in Scotland and England, in the days when a shovel was a shovel and McAlpine's fusiliers were the blood, sweat and tears rehearsal for the money-spinning lyric. Their music too — of its place, with pedigree in style, eclecticism and technique — has also passed through the filter of the days of Paddy in the Smoke, yet they remain true to home teaching, with a classicism that absorbs outside influence: as with 'The Marine Jig', which was composed in Edinburgh by an 1880s Irish dancing master, learned by the migrant Donegal workers and brought home to the Croaghs. There is the 'Maggie Pickens' too, and 'The Moneymusk' — a striking conversion from the strathspey to the high-rhythm, house-dance variant, 'The Highland'. The Campbells have personal style too, a great deal of which is inherited and preserved from their father, Peter, a close associate of the great travelling fiddlers Johnny Doherty and his brothers, who 'stopped' regularly in the family home.

The family come from the townland of Tangaveane in the glen on the ascent up to the Croaghs' 2219 feet. 'There was a whole lot of musicians in that townland,' says Vincent, who was born in 1938. 'It wasn't isolated in my time – there was houses all along and people living only a small little piece apart.' Their father, Peter, was a noted fiddler, as was his father, James. Like Vincent and Jimmy, Peter had spent a portion of his life working in another culture – in America. Missing the society and culture of home often gives the economic exile a heightened appreciation of everything to do with it, especially music, and ever since Peter's return, his home has been the premier music house in central Donegal.

House-dances and playing for pleasure were the regime. An open door brought in the Dohertys on their peregrinations. His sons Vincent, Jimmy and Columba played from an early age, and his brother Josie became his – and the Croaghs' – living archive: he can lilt and play not only the local repertoire but its variations too. When Peter's brothers play in public, they are not satisfied unless he gives them his approval. Such attention to detail is these days labelled pedantry, and, in the eyes and ears of predatory superficiality, it would be deemed 'purism'. Yet, no previously uninformed observer could fail to be impressed and moved by the sheer reasonability of Vincent and Jimmy Campbell's superb ear and aesthetic interest in accuracy, change and difference – the art of music making.

They give pride of place to an all-points-alertness in the process of social music making and an emotional interest in its people as people. They play in a style transmitted from another generation by a process vastly superior to any digital technology, a process honed by Vincent's compulsive collecting and searching out on his bicycle in younger days. In the physical terrain of his childhood, this was no lesser a feat than the Tour de France! Yet none of his musical knowledge is lofty or arrogant. A life of music is full of travel, new experience and sheer good *craic* and, while such may be true of any small place, it was a triumph in the Croaghs in the remote, dark days before mass transport and electricity.

Memories of pranks pepper the reminiscences of these musicians. Like the tale of their grandfather from Silver Hill who, with a friend, pretended someone was dead so they could collect funeral 'dues' on his behalf, in order to buy drink for themselves. 'There was some characters going! There was mighty things done! You see there was one person who would give out hell, and then there was a few more who would enjoy it. And they wouldn't let the thing go any further themselves, because there was some little bit of fun in it.'

Vincent learned to play when he was young: 'We were never taught, only my father would learn us a couple of simple tunes first and then he would let you carry on from that. Then you'd learn from other fiddle players. There was a lot of house-dances going at that time. People would come home from America and go away again, and they held what they called "convoys". That was a night of music and dance. And you would be playing with the other fiddle players any chance you'd get. So you learned. There was an awful lot of dances, you see, in this part of the country.'

Vincent Campbell's mother was also from the Croaghs; she didn't play, but she danced. House-dances were the community's social outlet before the war, and these came in all kinds to suit all sizes of kitchen. 'There was a big set and a small set. It was only in a big kitchen you'd ever see a sixteen-hand reel. But they had these other dances, small ones, so that everybody could dance. They had a clap dance – "Tugadh na Lámh" – and the "Maggie Pickey" the step dance and the hornpipe. They danced the reel as well.' Footwork was important in all of these, especially in the reel: 'There was a figure eight in it. They would let hands go, d'you see, every other bar or so in the "Barnas Mór Reel", and they done this step dance every one of them on their own and then they would join the hands again, go around again. The tune they used to play for that was "The Wind that Shakes the Barley".'

Fiddle was the main instrument. It was common enough for people to have the chance to learn how to play. And with tunes in constant exercise for dancing, everyone recognised or could lilt them. 'Every house you went into there'd be only a few that hadn't a fiddle. It was a common thing to have two to three fiddles in a house.' Mostly the fiddles were professionally made – brought back from Scotland – but sometimes there might be almost flawless replicas made locally from tea-chest plywood by a 'handy carpenter', or perhaps from sheet brass by a tinsmith such as with the fiddle-playing Dohertys.

Fiddles were in constant circulation, aided by the travelling tinsmiths. These were semi-professional musicians who travelled and played their own circuits, where they learned a wider repertoire. 'There was a lot of fiddles that came with the Dohertys, swapped. They would buy a fiddle here now, or they would give their own fiddle for a pound, maybe ten shillings at that time, maybe five shillings. They'd swap their fiddle for what they called "a swap and a boot".' Or they might buy a fiddle from one house, work on it – repairing cracks, changing the stain, moving the soundpost and adjusting the strings – and sell it to a neighbour, who wouldn't know it was the same fiddle. This process was seen as quite mystical. There were hints of how it was done, rumours were spread – or even, perhaps, red herrings were laid by the Dohertys. Famous is the tale of the woodstain made from the red dye of the Lifebuoy soap carton!

Fiddle may have been the most popular instrument in 'the glen', but an uncle of Vincent's played the melodeon too, and his cousins played tin whistle. 'Another relation, Hughie Campbell, he played the pipes. He used to play with Johnny Doran, and I mind him and Johnny together at Brocagh fair swapping tunes – and playing on each other's pipes too! Then up where I come from they played, you know, the Jew's harp – they could play it for dancers. The 'trump', they used to call it here. Hughie McMonagle was a master. If anybody was going to Scotland, he would land at that house if he heard about it the night before and they would tell him when they were coming back. And they would bring him back a trump. And he ended up with the two beams in the house covered with trumps! They were the old type, completely differently made. They were a lot bigger than the ordinary ones. They could make far more music you know — they were louder.' Sadly, McMonagle's trump collection has been lost.

Donegal's most travelled and famous fiddler was Hugh Gillespie from nearby Ballybofey. He went to America in 1928. He was sponsored by Michael Coleman and broadcast on local radio with him for the then phenomenal fee of $55 per hour, in the process adopting and becoming expert in the 'Sligo' style. He recorded half a dozen 78 records playing with the Star of Erin Orchestra and he played in Carnegie Hall too. Part of his legacy is his — unusual then — preference for guitar accompaniment. Vincent's father had been a near neighbour of Gillespie in Ireland and played with him at the many house-dances during his nine years of working in America. Travelling first to Regina in Canada with the free emigration scheme of 1927, Peter had smuggled his way into the States in an orange-bin on a fruit lorry to meet with his wife-to-be. Her family had also been musical; they were singers. There had been little time for learning music skills, for all twelve in the family had been sent out to hire at a young age — Vincent's mother at the age of nine: 'They would send them out to some neighbouring people that they knew — so she was hired to a place for two years — and then they were sent back to school after that for another two years. That was the system. Girls at that time, if they only had three months with the parish priest they had a better chance of getting a reference.' The reference could get work in America, and so she went, at the age of twenty-two, and was married there at twenty-four. 'They were in America at the time of the Depression. She worked in a convent there for a good while and her job was giving out soup in a soup kitchen.'

Immediate post-war life in the Croaghs was hard too, and people were constantly migrating for work — often also to avoid the harshness of winter at home. For Vincent and many others, from their late teens on, Glasgow, with its strong Donegal population, was a popular destination. 'When I was eighteen and a half I went to work as an apprentice carpenter in Stephens' shipyard. Nine months I was there. Then I went up to the Highlands, to Glenlyon, to work on the hydroelectric dam.' Forecasts of snow drove them south to London in 1958.

In the 1950s, London was 5% Irish, many of them new immigrants rebuilding the city and developing the road system. They were far from community censure, had money to spend on leisure, and a portion of that was in the pub. The desire for sounds of the homeland was strong, and so a semi-professionalism emerged among musicians, who gathered for Sunday-morning — and sometimes all-week —

sessions in the bars of north London, most iconically the Favourite in Holloway. Vincent, who was a plasterer himself, was back in Donegal by 1962, then he went to Dublin, married Margaret Gantly and lived in County Meath. He worked on the Gaeltacht offices in Rathcarn for a year, then on the building of the factory there. 'When I went in there first there was no music nearly in pubs at all, and we started, myself and Joe Toland. Then I used to play on my own, and with Patsy Parks, a step dancer and *céilí* dancer from Manorhamilton. Begod, before I left Meath, every pub in Meath, nearly, had music!'

In 1978 Vincent returned to Glenties to build and farm. The music revival brought musicians like Dr Billy Loughnane and Joe Cooley to the Glen Tavern and fans to Vincent's door, younger musicians eager to learn like Dermot McLaughlin and the Glackins. However, despite playing the music of other areas – learned in Scotland, England, Dublin and Meath – his passion was always for the local. He sought out players, tunes and versions, and absorbed the details of various techniques. Particularly interesting were the Doherty brothers who had filled his childhood years: 'They had their own way of bowing. They had their own way of playing, their own way of fingering, that'll never be got again – never. We got a lot of it, but I would say that, you know, you would nearly have to be born a Doherty to do it. They had what they call their own stuff – as well as Skinner's and Coleman's.'

Now in his late fifties, Vincent is a conscious keeper of the music of central Donegal and the legacy of the Dohertys. His father Peter still plays at the age of 90, and is still enthusiastic about upcoming younger players and visitors who follow the Donegal-repertoire group Altan. Tape recorders and CDs may give time, notation and rhythm, but only the local ambience can give the music its fourth dimension of thrill and magic. Vincent has recorded on several albums, as has Jimmy, but it is their playing in a kitchen, or on Saturdays in the Glen Tavern, that generates meaning.

Paddy Canny

BY FINTAN VALLELY

Back in 1919, the island of Ireland was but a province of Britain, and the garrison of 43,000 British troops deployed on the streets and roads of Munster, Leinster, Connacht and Ulster were costing the London exchequer £860,000 each month. Into this momentous turbulence Paddy Canny was born on the ninth of September that year, at Glendree in east County Clare, above the town of Tulla on the road to Gort. His father, Pat, was reared there and his mother, Catherine McNamara, came from Feakle.

Born in 1886, his father, Pat Canny, was one of the best fiddlers of his time. He had learned from blind Paddy McNamara, a music teacher and a fiddler of note. Pat 'kept' Paddy Mac between November and February of each year in order that he could teach some of the neighbours' children, and six or seven of Pat's friends – like Tommy McNamara, Mick Donoghue, Patrick Moloney and Paddy Hayes. It was almost like a school – they attended to learn and they all played together. In the spring 'they'd make a little collection for Mac and return him back to his base at Cooleen Bridge!'

'Cooleen Bridge' is the title of a reel in Francis O'Neill's 1907 Chicago collection of Irish music, and indeed Pat Canny's other influence was Johnny Allen, who had given this tune and 'The Maids of Feakle' to O'Neill when he was around the area. Pat Canny also taught neighbouring children and friends, and through this Paddy himself learned: 'This girl was coming and she was from down the road. Cathy McNamara was her name. I suppose I was eight or nine. I was doing the lessons from school and they'd be sitting down there and I'd be doing the lessons at the table and of course I was watching the music more than I was watching the lessons. I have an idea my father had shown me a few little bits all right – on the Clarke's whistle, the black one. There was one in every house in those days; you'd buy them for fourpence. But I'd make sure I had the tune as good as her by the time she went home!'

His brothers Jack and Mickey both played too, but Paddy had the greater enthusiasm. Quick at picking things up, he was on to the fiddle at the age of ten. Greatly encouraged by his father, he was completely absorbed in music as a youngster, stealing time from agricultural commitments to learn tunes wherever he could hear them, or from notes scribbled down by people like Feakle piper and fiddler Martin Rochford.

Influence and inspiration had to be largely local, as players from other areas were scarce and seasonal. The area was not on the rounds of the travelling pipers Johnny and Felix Doran, but they did come as far as Martin Rochford near Feakle. The Dunnes were another family Paddy would see playing at the Galway Races each year. A lot of people sang – notably Danny Connors – mostly ballads, particularly at the house-dances. Irish speaking was defunct in the area in Paddy's time, but his father had some.

Reels and jigs were the tunes played in Paddy's younger days, and some of the set dances which were made popular by Francis O'Neill's music collection. Paddy read music, but

preferred to learn from memory, or a recording. Fiddles were the most popular instrument. The flute was scarce, but there were concertinas: 'Mostly men played concertina here, but there was the odd woman here and there. If the dance was in their own house they'd probably have a go, but they wouldn't ever follow it up that much.'

His teenage years in the 1930s were the last abandoned fling of the house-dance and crossroads dance before morals, fashion and legislation began sealing them up in history's pages. There were weddings, too, to be played for, and seasonal and emigration ritual dances: 'There was a string of them from one end of the year to the other. A lot of the local girls went to England, as you know, and they got holidays every year and when they came home then there was one scene of dancing every night. And then the next thing somebody else would arrive at some other local house again and the same thing happened. When I was young, I was mad for that kind of thing!'

Glendree indeed had a reputation as a great place for dancing. At dances in the local school, musicians played in shifts – Sandy Carthy (concertina) and Bill Malley (fiddle) for three or four sets at a time, then Paddy with 'Pack' Holohan (concertina) for three or four more. 'We kept an awful lot of the dances going like that. There didn't seem to be any scarcity of players then. Maybe they'd come in from outside.' This seems to have been a turn-around from the previous generation's experience: 'In my father's time he was often called out of the bed to go to play at a house-dance or maybe a wedding or an American wake – and he got up out of the bed and went! And there was no bobs [fees] for musicians in that earlier time either!'

The standard house in those years had a big kitchen in the middle, smaller rooms at either end, and maybe a loft. Dancing would involve just four couples at a time and, when they stopped, four more might continue on the same tune. Big crowds could be accommodated in that way, all dancing for a short time in turn. This was the currency of socialising and entertainment right through to the 1940s, and part of the hunting of the wren ritual – the 'Wran'. Nine or ten lads would be out on it over Christmas Day and Stephen's Day. Dancing would follow on the second day, perhaps in the school. 'After two days out hunting for the wren, a lot of the lads weren't able for the dance!'

With the demise of house-dancing all over the country, the enterprising clergy went on to organise dances, legally, in the schools to raise parish funds. 'Sets' had been the currency of house-dancing, but, with the change to halls, céilí dances and old-time waltzes were introduced too. Dance continued to be the pulse of local life. Travel then was on foot, or bicycle, but roads weren't tarred and, particularly in winter, were often so stony as to be dangerous to cycle, particularly with an instrument strapped to your back. At a distance of sixty-three years, this hectic pattern of small-audience music-making seems like a romantic idyll, but no doubt it took its toll on work hours, and one of the desired effects of the new legislation was to whip the new nation into line: ''Twas all much better for the health!' says Paddy.

The dance halls took with one hand, but they gave with the other. Bigger venues demanded louder music. This, céilí dance promotion and the fashion created by 'jazz' bands prompted musicians to get together in groups. In 1946, Paddy Canny and others got together a band to compete in Féile Luimní. Joe Cooley and P. Joe Hayes were involved too. They won the competition, their reputation was instantly established, and so was born the Tulla Céilí Band. Formal dress was part of the style. The members of the band changed according to availability, agricultural cycles and human crises, but a central 'sound' managed to survive – even to the present day.

A series of live, fifteen-minute Radio Éireann broadcasts followed for Paddy at the end of the decade. His playing of 'Trim the Velvet', in fact, was used as the signature tune for Ciarán Mac Mathúna's *Job of Journeywork* programme for several years – a great honour for a player then. His reputation enhanced that of the band, and the engagements soon became almost too much. He was in demand on his own, too, but a shyness dogged him. 'There'd be odd concerts and I couldn't face them at all. My trouble in my young days, and even up to later, was my shyness – I couldn't face a crowd if I had to go out on the stage. But now, in my old age, of course it is different – I don't take that much notice! But in them days if I was asked to play I'd nearly ask a couple of lads maybe to stand in front of me. It had an awful effect on me.'

Shyness was reserved for solo playing; Paddy enjoyed the band. Relations were good, the travelling was interesting and the money was attractive, but, 'If you were drinking a couple of pints of Guinness and smoking a few cigarettes, 'twas all gone in a couple of nights.' Married to Philomena Hayes in 1961, the arrival of his daughters Rita and Mary after 1964 brought other responsibilities and he gave up playing out. 'There was a herd of cows to be milked in the morning, and there was a little bit of a crop to be put down, turf to be cut.' During those quiet years he would play with people who called to the house – in particular Peadar O'Loughlin.

A trip to America with Dr Bill Loughnane in 1956 resulted in Paddy, P. Joe Hayes and Peadar O'Loughlin making a recording: 'Peter Hunt's studio was booked and we were to be there of a Friday evening to do whatever we had to do. As far as I know, Peadar O'Loughlin got a loan of Seán Reid's car to go to Dublin. The three of us went up and we got Bridie Lafferty – she was to back us on the piano – and we landed into the studio. We had only some couple of takes done, but, at around eleven or twelve o'clock at night, he announced that that was it, he was closing down for the night and 'if you could come back on Monday'. Well there we were, we had the loan of the car, we had a few bob in our pockets and, I suppose, if we had to stay over we had enough for a couple of nights anyway. We

looked at each other and we said nothing and came away out. Wherever we were staying, we had our chat and we decided that we'd look for a studio in the morning and we got one! We went in and we weren't too long at it either and we all played our few tunes without even a rehearsal of what we were going to do and we put them on two tapes and that was it!' The recording – *All Ireland Champions* – is regarded now as one of the classics of traditional music.

Up to the 1960s, session playing was scarce. All music was for a purpose, for dancing. Travel with the band introduced Paddy to players from other places – like Fred Finn and Peter Horan from near Kilavil, County Sligo. But Paddy disliked the public house as a venue: ''Tis all grand for half an hour or an hour, till they get steamed up and make too much noise and then you don't know what's happening. The pubs to me are a dead loss, nowadays anyway. The louder you play, the louder they talk, then when the tune is over you stop – and they stop. Then you play again and they all begin.'

America, of course, was the birthplace of the session. In an alien culture people paid attention to music that, over there, they were obliged to treasure: 'The only place I saw a good session was in New York when we were there. We used to have all the lads around – Joe Cooley, Larry Redican, Andy McGann, Paddy Reynolds and Paddy O'Brien.'

Paddy's music has a characteristic 'lonesome' touch, something that he feels has developed in his own playing rather than coming from his father. He met regularly with

John Kelly in Dublin, and visited Tommy Potts too, a man who 'had his own ideas about tunes and music', but 'nearly went too far away some of the times from the tune'. Paddy does not play slow airs: 'I never did, I couldn't have the patience somehow!'

His own daughters don't play, but his grandchild is presently learning from concertina player Mary McNamara. Paddy Canny is not impressed by modern trends in traditional music. He doesn't go out much these days, the music comes to him – friends drop in and play. In 1997, aged 78, he made a superb recording, which is packed with all his eclecticism and faraway nostalgia. With years to catch up on, he considers he has the material for more. Retired from farming, he and Philomena look after their grandchildren every afternoon. 'I do little jobs around the place, drive the tractor and saw a bit of timber that's knocked by the wind. I come in and play a few tunes – and that's about our lifestyle at the moment!'

Liz Carroll

BY FINTAN VALLELY

To talk of 'regional' styles of Irish instrumental music is to talk of the fiddle. Between them, the major Donegal, Sligo, east Galway, west Clare and Sliabh Luachra 'sounds' share fingering, bowing, dynamics, demeanour and repertoire. Musicians in strong Irish areas abroad also have their own sound, such as the music of 1950s London and that of the United States. Liz Carroll was born into such an exile community in the US, living a childhood involving a constant awareness of Irishness that the Irish in Ireland have rarely any call to even consider and can afford the luxury of scorning. She shares a plaintive 'call' in her fiddle music with east-coast compatriots Lad O'Beirne, Larry Redican, Ed Reavy and local Johnny McGreevy. Listen to her peeling off the layers of emotion in 'Jackson's Reel', digging into the ecstatic sadness of the slightly named 'Pigeon on the Gate', twisting a rambling *sugán* in 'Wynding the Hay', rendering the jaunty nostalgia of 'The Setting Sun' and the flamboyant concentration of 'The Road to Recovery': her fiddling is powerfully impressive and 'of its place', but cut too from her very own eclectic cloth.

Liz Carroll was born on the Chicago south-side in 1956. Her father Kevin, a carpenter, comes from Brocca, on the Birr side of Tullamore, County Offaly. An accordion player himself, he spent his younger years (before his exile in 1951) travelling between house-dances with the box on his bike. Liz's mother, Eileen, is from Ballyhahill, near Shanagolden in west Limerick; her own father, Tom Cahill, played fiddle. Initially she started work at the first available job – a rectory cook – then she became a bank cashier, where she discovered a skill with figures. She was the eldest of fifteen and had gone out to an uncle and aunt in Chicago; Liz's father was the youngest of fourteen and had gone out to his brothers. The two met at a dance in one of Chicago's many Irish dance halls, where the fare was old-time Irish waltzes, *céilí* and songs.

Living in the States in the post-war years meant the possibility of holiday visits to Ireland, something which previous generations of emigrants had been denied. And so Liz Carroll's family visited 'home', first when she was five and again when she was ten. Once she started playing and dancing, they returned regularly and she took part in *fleadhanna* and competitions, sometimes twice in the one year, all through the 1970s. A step dancer as well – with the Dennehy School – Liz was often back in Ireland for world championships and the Oireachtas – playing fiddle. This was also the school that Michael Flatley was part of – he was in all their choreographies. Indeed, Liz remembers the original 'Lord of the Dance' as the Dennehy School's show in which Flatley played the lead role of none other than Jesus. 'He was the one that died. He would hang on the cross with his head down, the music would stop and we'd go into an air!'

Her father played accordion a lot, and the instrument was always around the house. Learning on that she was on her own, for Kevin had his own way: 'He learns a tune by osmosis. He just puts his fingers over the keyboard and,

after many hours, the tune comes out. But if I tell him, "Dad, just stop there and play just that one note," he really can't do that. So he didn't teach me! But he played the music, and I found it.' She took up fiddle at nine, lucky that in her school (Visitation) Sister Francine taught piano and violin. 'That was pretty darn rare in south-side Chicago! When she realised I could play, she asked me to bring in the accordion.'

It was piano that Liz really wanted to play, but fate was against it. 'My parents bought me an upright piano, but we were on the second floor of an apartment building at the time. We couldn't get it up the back and we couldn't get it up the front. With the frustration of having to return it to the shop, my mom said, "Why don't you just try the fiddle? Grandpa plays it. You can't take a piano around with you. A fiddle you can take anywhere." So that's what I did.' Violin lessons followed, first practising the fingering on a stick, and learning to keep the bow in place with another. 'As soon as I got a fiddle I just loved it. I could have easily missed it!'

'Right away my folks really liked the music, because my dad played and my mom's father played. That was a great connection for the two of them. When we were little, before I ever played, we used to be going out to hear music. So when I started playing they called up the Irish Musicians' Association and said "Where do you meet and can we bring our daughter?" Funny enough, that hadn't happened with the accordion – they never called about that!'

Competitions were not part of her early playing life,

although she has one trophy from a *fleadh cheoil* in Chicago in 1966: 'But it was interesting because, at it, Kevin Keegan and Eleanor Neary were in one band, and Johnny McGreevy and Joe Cooley were in another.' Liz had a good ear: 'All I had to do was sit back at the session, no pressure, nothing – just playing the tunes. I'd come back the next week and they were playing the same tunes again so I could just pick it up.' Such repetition is typical of session playing. Apart from being useful for learners, it gives space for music to be expressed in different tempos and moods too. The urge to learn new tunes led her to learn to write down the music. 'If you were at a session and you'd want to remember a tune you'd just heard and you didn't want it to be killing you for the rest of the night. So I started writing whole notes down on a sheet of paper, just so I could remember the start of the tune. Then I got good at it.'

Fleadhanna were an excuse to travel to Ireland, and so Liz and her parents went to Listowel in 1973. 'I was scared to death, because I didn't even know how people played in New York, let alone Ireland.' But meeting and playing regularly with Balbriggan accordion player Paddy Gavin in Hoban's pub in Chicago one summer had encouraged her. Aged just sixteen, she came second: 'I was surprised that I got anything, I played so slow. I had played slow because Paddy had said, "You'll get nervous, so play slow because you'll really play faster than that." The thing was – I didn't!' She came back the following year, smitten by the freedom and energy of the street sessions. 'And it was a chance to visit relatives, even though we didn't really have the money.' In 1974 she came first in the under-18, and in 1975 she won the senior too. By then she hated the pressure of it and, having climbed her personal mountain, never competed again.

Liz Carroll is as well known as a composer as a player, this skill beginning almost as an exercise the first week she had the fiddle. 'Composing tunes for me, being in Chicago, was just boredom. You'd learned all the tunes you could get – and you know how slowly records were coming out in those years. I think I was just looking for something different to do with my fingers. My tunes are more melodic now than they used to be.' Tune-making came under different circumstances. Once she had to write a tune out on the windscreen of her VW beetle. 'Other times you just hear one little bit of something and you don't find what goes with it for a long time. Or at the piano you hit a few chords and you go "that's nice, that's nice" and you build a tune around that. Some of them are made on the fiddle, some on the accordion. Some of the tunes are made with different instruments in mind.'

Liz studied social psychology at university and then elementary education. In the early 1980s she got a job teaching 13- to 14-year-olds. This was not her idea of a life: 'Oh my God, what a nightmare!' She played in Washington DC for a summer, and then a State Department tour to Africa with Mick Moloney got her out of teaching in 1983. Summer festivals and winter classes and workshops have kept her busy teaching fiddle at all levels ever since. Trian, with Dáithí Sproule and Billy McComiskey (accordion), is her best-known group. She writes for theatre productions, and occasional snatches too for radio and television. In 1985 she married cabinet maker Charles Lacey, whom she had met through his blues harmonica playing, and they now have two children.

Tall and leanly healthy, Liz Carroll is passionate about sports too – baseball, American football and basketball. In this she makes up for lost time, as when she was at school such unbecoming pastimes were forbidden for girls: 'Now I'm always out shooting baskets with the kids.' Her eleven-year-old son Patrick plays trumpet at school, and nine-year-old Alison plays saxophone. She doesn't believe in influencing them, but: 'I told them recently "I'm gonna teach you guys for two weeks. Just so as you have a notion of what I'm doing. Would you like that?" And they said "Sure, Mom." I always put the kids into things that I never got to do – they can ice skate, go to swimming lessons. But I think they feel that music is right here anyway, all around them. They go around the house humming tunes. If they really want it, they'll go for it.'

Liz finds some of the modern developments in traditional music 'very interesting': 'more of it is good than not'. She feels that, while a lot of it is not to her taste, if it has an audience, 'why not? When it's all over, the same people can sit down and play older tunes in a session and still enjoy it.' She is impressed by Séamus Egan's group,

Solas. 'You could be just rolling along playing the tune and they can pick a melody underneath it and play it at half speed. That kind of stuff, it's good. It really sets an incredibly different atmosphere.'

Still, she strongly feels herself to be an individual. 'I heard a lot of blues here in Chicago, but I never fell into that style of playing. I'm much more interested in the fiddle-y type of stuff. So it's still Irish, what I'm doing. But I really like Texas swing, old-time music, probably if anything just little hints of jazz.' Chords interest her: 'the accordion in me'. She might indeed shock her friends and make a recording on it. She admires good rock and rap recordings, 'when it gets into a real groove. Maybe that's because I really like the dancing, and pushing a dancer along.' She likes French-Canadian and Cape Breton music, the Montreal-based band La Bottine Souriante, with their mixing of reels and brass, she finds 'fabulous'.

Liz Carroll feels that she is now 'coming into her prime', with ideas of what to do, and the confidence to do it: 'I'm sitting on a ton of tunes and I've never made a book out of them. I could be dead tomorrow and what would have been the point? Nobody would even know where they are!' She has written between 125 and 150 of these, mostly before her children were born, and always 'only as the spirit moved' her. Rearing her children is her priority, this allowing her only meagre time to tour, but, as the millennium dawns, it is new technology and a bigger market for Irish music that she sees as her opportunity to make her second definitive album. Recognition of all her outstanding work in teaching, and indeed playing, all over the US came in 1994, when she received the prestigious National Endowment for the Arts National Heritage Award. Previous recipients have been singer Joe Heaney (1982), fiddler Martin Mulvihill (1984), Michael Flatley (1988) and Jack Coen (1991). Says Liz Carroll, 'I'm very proud of that!'

Joe Cooley

BY CHARLIE PIGGOTT

Portait opposite is of Jack Cooley, brother of Joe

For many, the year 1973 will be remembered for Ireland's entry to the European Economic Community and as the year of a major oil crisis when petrol shortages and long dreary queues signalled the stark realisation of our dependence on oil. However, in the traditional music calendar, the year is sadly marked with the loss of two of Ireland's finest traditional musicians, Willie Clancy and Joe Cooley. Clancy died in January and Cooley in December. Both musicians were tradesmen, carpenter and block-layer respectively, and for them good fun and good music making were the order of the day. 'They loved life and they loved their music', as one commentator put it. Their lives were inextricably linked: west Clare rambling houses, the Tulla Céilí Band, London's heady days of traditional music in the 1950s and music making together at the renowned Galway Races. Today, their music is still celebrated in the western villages of Milltown Malbay and Gort.

Joe Cooley was born in 1924 near Peterswell, County Galway, close to the northern boundary of the Sliabh Aughty mountains. Music and song abounded in the Cooley family, but Joe and his brother Séamus would become the more famous members. Joe was a wanderer, continually compelled to seek out the company of other musicians, from whom he absorbed new tunes and new music. He worked and performed in Clare, Dublin and London and, on emigrating to the United States in 1954, settled in various cities including New York, Boston, Chicago and San Francisco. This wandering brings to mind the peregrination of the early Irish monks: the self-imposed exile intended to create sadness, loneliness and sorrow, experienced through a yearning for home. Whether Joe's exilic wanderings were consciously linked to pathos in his music or not is debatable but, like the music of Pádraig O'Keeffe, Martin Rochford, Junior Crehan and other contemporaries, Joe Cooley's music possessed a strong element of *draíocht.*

Draíocht means spell, enchantment or uncanny ingenuity, and one of the words for a magician in Irish is *draoi* (hence 'druid'); the initial letters dr in many Irish words seem to imply magic of some kind (e.g. *dreoilín*). The music collector Brendan Breathnach once stated that 'a high quality of the traditional musician is his ability to draw a fine lonesome reel out of his instrument' a feat which is easier to accomplish in a minor key than in a major one. To a large extent, Cooley's music was played in major keys and, against the odds, he consistently created *ceol draíochta.*

Many observers and musicians consider Joe Cooley's music to be special — something to do with his blending of the elements of spirited lift and plaintiveness. Highs and lows, the tears of joy, are evident simultaneously, a communion of opposites in psychological terms. Bryan MacMahon once asked the writers Seán Ó Faoláin and Frank O'Connor for advice on short-story writing and the reply came: take a female idea and a male idea, put them together and the children are short stories. Bryan thought it a joke, but when he examined what he had been told he found it a most profound statement. He would use this marriage of opposites for many of his own short stories.

Cooley's Reel

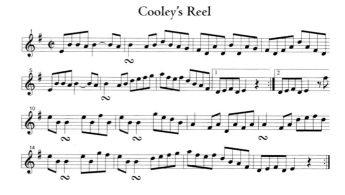

A tune which occupies a prime position in the repertoire of many Irish traditional musicians and is most often associated with the Cooley brothers is 'Cooley's Reel'. Though sometimes linked to Joe's music, the emergence of this fine piece of music derives from a combined effort and demonstrates how many tunes found expression in the pre-tape recorder age. Séamus dates its origin to the 1940s, when, still in their teens, he and Joe attended a house session in the adjoining county of Clare. An old man with a battered-looking concertina sat playing in front of an open fire (some of the missing buttons had been replaced with cigarette ends!) and a particular tune which he was playing caught their fancy. Come what may, on returning home, they could not remember the tune but sat up in bed till daybreak whistling and humming until finally a bold reel emerged. Joe took credit for the first part and Séamus had recomposed the turn of the tune. It has been played and performed ever since as 'Cooley's Reel'.

Joe Cooley and the other great accordion player, Paddy O'Brien from Nenagh, played for a time together in the Tulla Céilí Band in the early 1950s and it is said that the music was fine. They teamed up later in the decade in New York and, again, according to Woodford flute player Jack Coen, the reverence with which they treated their music was remarkable. They appeared to instinctively understand the pace and key-setting for each tune, the *nós* or way wrapped up in the word tradition. For them the word did not simply imply the handing down of a melody but embraced simultaneously the attendant knowledge of how a tune should be handled. Each melody has a pulse and, as a friend of mine would say, 'everything finds its own level': tunes, poems, people and mountain streams. There's a story told to this day around the Sliabh Aughty mountains in south Galway concerning Joe Cooley playing for a dancer.

It was a time when farmers big and small
Had come to thrashing the harvest
The stacks of corn would be made in rows
And the thrashing machine would drive between them
A machine would need about fifteen helpers
To do the work smoothly
And the feeding of the machine
Was the most important and dangerous

The helper that would be throwing the sheaves of corn
Onto the platform of the machine
Would need to put the butts of the corn to the back
And put the seed to the front
It was very important
Only to give it
The way the man that was feeding the machine
Was able to take it

Now a special man
Used come from the west every year
To do the job of feeding the machine
And at that time after the day's work
There would be a dance in the house
And this man from the west
Was a good sean nós dancer
And the door of the house
Was lifted off the bucháns
And left on the kitchen floor
He stood up on the door
And Joe Cooley took out his accordion to play
And Joe said to him 'What way
Did you want the music?'
'Give it to me,' the man said
'According as I'm able to take it.'

TOMÁS Ó NIALLÁIN

Herein lay the bond between musician and dancer which produced the magic. They loved to dance to Cooley's music:

all the way from Castledaly down to Kilenena. The piper and fiddle player Martin Rochford tells me that Cooley had a different tempo. The dancers in that region would loosen the steel tips on their boots to enable them to step out the rolls and triplets when dancing to his music. They understood the music and vied with each other to step, dance and batter to every note of each tune and each note of every triplet. On a recent *cuairtíocht* to Bodyke with *bodhrán* player Tomás Ó Nialláin, the conversation, between tunes, drifted and focused on Cooley.

C.P.   *Tell me about the Kilenena lad who loved to dance to Cooley's music.*

M.R.   *Dinnie Coffey. He'd have a loose tip and he was able to drrr . . . drrr . . . drrr . . . along the floor. Yeah, every note of it with the tip and Cooley playing. With a good player he'd buzz along the floor.*

T.O.N.   *He'd slide from the front door to the back door.*

M.R.   *That's him. Now you have him.*

T.O.N.   *And he'd be knocking sparks out of the flags.*

M.R.   *Knocking sparks out of the flag with the tip.*

C.P.   *And was he the only one who would loosen the tip?*

M.R.   *There was more of them up there, too.*

T.O.N.   *He was the best of them up around there.*

M.R.   *Oh, he was. Cooley had that style of playing too, you know. They were able to dance to it around Peterswell, back Derrybrien, back Lough Mountain and Derrygoolin. Oh, they wouldn't miss a note.*

T.O.N.   *They used to be playing beyond there in Derrybrien in a very small place and be able to take out the range, take it out in the yard. Four or five of them mountainy ol' lads. Sure, 'twas only like a biscuit tin to them. And they'd dance like hell. They'd be sweating, they'd be black with sweat, coming out of it. They'd leave the range in then for the* bean a' tí [*woman of the house*] *at daybreak or whatever hour they'd break up.*

M.R.   *Cooley had them reels that were able to suit them. In fact, there wouldn't be a note lost on them. They wouldn't lose a note.*

In 1972, Joe Cooley returned to his native Peterswell from San Francisco. Followers of his music travelled from far and near, as Tony MacMahon writes, 'to hear the last great blast of *ceol*'. I feel privileged to have spent time with him, his friend Des Mulkere and his brother Jack one October evening in Finnerty's of Tubber. As I remember, the small crowded bar room was in semi-darkness but the energy from Joe Cooley's music was radiant. I'm told that, in some venues in San Francisco, people would sense on entering that Cooley was either expected in to play or had just left the premises having already played. Such was the effect of his personality and music.

Sean nós

*It's as natural
as the blue flowered scabious
no tricks or frills
that aren't incidental
to the origin.
Cooley had it.
For the spirit of* sean nós
*pervaded the darkest borders
of his music.*

ROGER LEACH

Lucy Farr

BY FINTAN VALLELY

Lucy Farr was born on 4 December, 1911, the year of the foundation of the Irish women's suffrage movement and Delia Larkin's Irish Women Workers' Union. This was just two days before the passing of legislation permitting women to take part in county councils. In a childhood dominated by women, Lucy took up fiddle and played in the dying years of the house-dance circuit. Working as a nurse in London during the war further developed a strongly independent spirit, as did losing her husband in 1971. Playing with The Rakes in England took her all over Britain. On visits to Ireland, she distinctly saw herself as a woman playing in the – then male-dominated – 'east Galway' tradition, and is regarded as having 'an old-fashioned fiddle style' that she has never changed.

Born at Baunyknave, Ballinakill, midway between Woodford and Loughrea in County Galway, Lucy was a Kirwan, one of the ancient fourteen tribes of Galway. She remembers her grandfather, Martin, as a great storyteller; he was also one of the original Fenians. Among her earliest recollections is seeing ten banners on staffs standing in front of the dresser on a Saturday night, in preparation for a Sunday morning parade: 'There was a fife-and-drum band – my father was in that. We used to walk up half a mile into this particular field and they would march around the field playing this lovely marching music, and back home again. The banners were the green, white and gold – this would have been around the time of the 1916 Rising, before the Black and Tans.'

Lucy had seven siblings, all but one of them girls. Her brother Martin is the last in the line, heir to the Kirwans' Seat near Caherlistrane: 'They were travellers; they used to do the silk route to China. There's still a lane in Galway with a sign reading 'Kirwan's Lane' after our family.' Her mother – from Abbey, Ballinakill – had no music, but, like Lucy, enjoyed great age and good health. A maiden aunt who lived with them played fiddle, and is fondly remembered for her party piece: 'We always had a full house of musicians and people in for *cuairt* [social visit]. She used to pick up the fiddle and play a little jig – she'd lilt it and dance it at the same time. I've tried my damnedest and I can't do it! Then she got married and left the fiddle behind and I've still got it.'

Her brother played the flute and sang, Lucy learned concertina and she and another sister sang too. She began playing at eight or nine, and picked up tunes by noodling at the fiddle on her own, corrected and complimented by her father. He played melodeon as well as flute for the dances in their kitchen. Lucy attended Duniry School, where the teacher – a cousin of her mother – had a harmonium and piano and grounded Lucy in tonic solfa, and taught her to identify pitch and to sing. Lucy's big desire was to acquire new tunes, and in particular to be able to read the music that she knew lay idling in the pages of Francis O'Neill's collection, which she had seen somewhere. 'I borrowed it twice from some address in Dublin. I copied down hundreds of jigs and reels and I learned to write the music.

It gave you an opportunity to get more tunes, because people didn't have tape recorders in those days and you had to either learn something by ear or else get this O'Neill book.' But she was more interested in playing, and in reaching the spirit of the music, 'so I packed it up. I thought it was much better to get something into your own head and play it in your own way.'

Throughout Lucy's younger years there was dancing. Families were big, and there were lots of relatives to call in. 'Our house would be a gathering house. Musicians came in every Saturday night and the dances were always the same – half sets and a full set. And then, if you had enough room, you'd have a sixteen-hand set.' Local lads in Lucy's own age group would play for the dances, for all around there were players. Piper Stephen Moloney, who started the Ballinakill Band with Tommy Whelan, was a neighbour. His was a music house too. His sister was a friend of Lucy's aunt, his daughter Alice used to sing with Lucy and his son Jim taught her tunes. Tommy's daughter Kathleen played the fiddle with Lucy at many of the dances. 'Farther up the road there were so many musicians it was unbelievable. Loads of flute players! There were very few women players at all, apart from Aggie White.'

By the time Lucy left for England at the age of 24, the house-dance was being undermined by new, enforced social practices and legislation. *The Furrow*, a Catholic magazine, raged about dances being 'occasions of sin', sectarian violence coloured Belfast and the political authorities feared funds were being raised for the IRA. Lucy is bitter about the transfer of recreation from home to parochial hall in the same period. 'The church took over. We weren't allowed to hold the house-dances anymore, and that was the most awful crime against the Irish music that anyone could do. The priests, you know, they were vicious then. Oh yes, they'd condemn the late nights for stopping people coming to mass on Sunday because they were "up all night the night before" playing this awful music. But it never stopped any of us coming to mass on a Sunday. In fact they wanted to open a parochial hall beside the local church and have everybody come there instead on a Saturday night to the dance and pay half a crown to come in!' But Lucy and others felt too that 'the music wasn't the same there as in a kitchen'. The moral policing annoyed them as young adults. 'When the dances were over, they had this awful habit – the priest had a stick and he would wander around trying to find courting couples! We used to make a joke out of it, but that's how it was.' Between one thing and another, 'they killed the house-dances, they killed the music'.

Parochial halls and suchlike created a need for bands. Father Larkin, the local curate, began using the Ballinakill school for dancing on Saturdays, and so began the Ballinakill Céilí Band. Her father's illness and early death obliged Lucy to work on the farm, and subsequently prompted her to go to train as a nurse. In 1936 a nun came over from England to recruit. Her mother paid an 'entrance fee' of £50 and Lucy went to London to work without salary for six months. Two of her sisters followed, going to different hospitals, and Lucy finished in Lewisham General before going 'out on the district'.

Lucy married a Londoner in 1940 while working in a military hospital in Kent: 'A great man and a great follower of the music. He loved it!' She spent the war years there, but 'packed it up then altogether until the children had left home'. Her two sons joined the Royal Air Force, were educated to third level there and now work in industry. Her daughter is a gymnast. None of them plays Irish music, although the boys were quite proficient on guitar. 'Patsy is married and she has two girls – and they're married with children, so I am a great-granny. They don't play the fiddle, any of them. Isn't it heartbreaking?'

After the war Lucy moved into the new social space created by the construction-trade Irish: 'The pubs started to open up and the pub where the music really started first was at the Elephant and Castle – and it was called the Favourite. Jimmy Power, a fiddler from Waterford, started up the sessions there with Reg Hall (piano) in 1950. And before long it was a venue for every musician in London on a Sunday morning.' Indeed, *Paddy in the Smoke* was the LP which came out of those sessions, and Lucy herself plays on four of its nostalgia-soaked tracks – with Bobby Casey, Jimmy Power and Andy O'Boyle. 'A lot of people didn't come in at first – it was a very sleazy sort of pub. But it became very very respectable, and you never knew who was going to turn up. The place was filled with musicians. Jimmy Power always made a point of trying to get everybody up on the stage – even if it was only to play one tune. Everybody got a chance.'

Lucy has composed tunes in her time too – a couple of slides and a couple of polkas written after the death of her husband in 1971. 'I was feeling very lonely, very fed up – sleepless nights because of the time I had spent at the hospital. At the back of the mind, half asleep and half awake, little snippets of notes used to come into my mind and I had the piano in the house at the time. I just tinkled out the notes, starting with the single jigs. The second one – I really got to like it. I thought, "That's not a bad tune at all!" I'll never forget that morning when I heard it coming over my little radio when I was lying there in bed. I thought, "Good God, that's my tune!" Then they said that it was Nollaig Casey and that she was playing two of "Brady's sets". Who's Brady? I never did find out. I thought it was rather nice that somebody played them. I was so chuffed!'

The 'Brady' was Paul Brady, whom Lucy knew from going around the folk clubs and from her twenty-five years playing with The Rakes. That group had Reg Hall on piano, Michael Plunkett on the fiddle and flute, and Paul Gross on the fiddle. They would play at festivals and clubs and the occasional Irish wedding party. Lucy often sang unaccompanied songs, like 'Matt Hyland', 'Sweet Inniscarra' and 'The Bantry Girl's Lament'. Once she went to Bill Leader's in Leeds to record, but got cold feet. 'I never thought I was good enough. You see, when I started it was

all men, there were so few lady fiddle players and you sort of felt that you shouldn't be there. That was the feeling I used to get when I was young. Not so much in our own house at home, because there were two or three girls who used to play fiddle. And it gave you a sort of a feeling of "What's wrong with us?" – and there was nothing wrong with us at all!' Shyness is still a common enough condition among traditional musicians. Unlike classical players, they are not taught to perform; they simply learn to play. 'I've never really got rid of my shyness where playing was concerned. I always feel I should have been playing a lot better. I didn't feel badly when I used to sing – I used to really let myself go.' The Rakes recorded and broadcast many times, and Lucy is on just one album.

Between working, rearing children and coping with a sick husband, Lucy drew back from music for some years. But by the mid-1960s she was going home for a month at a time, meeting and sessioning with Paddy Fahy (fiddle), Paddy Carty (flute), Paddy Doorey (fiddle), and Tony Molloy (flute) at her sister's in Loughrea. The music then shifted to Moylan's Hotel, and its Saturday night and Sunday sessions became legendary. All this Paddy Carty oversaw, ensuring fairness for all interested publicans.

Lucy is sceptical about the folk scene's popular idols. Like a lot of musicians at the time, she found them egotistical and unsympathetic. So too with the media personalities, who were too controlling; and she is critical of how they selected material. She sees no value in 'classical' training for youngsters in Irish music. 'I don't see the point in training young children to play Irish music – you don't need to! I've followed the life of the music and the musicians all through the years, but I still think that there is one little thing missing in all of them. They're not being told about their ancestry, and the feeling that you should have for your own traditional Irish music. That's lacking in a lot of the young players today. The "lonesome" touch is gone in the music, and that is a big, big pity.'

Living now in her own flat in a 'retirement block', Lucy Farr has privacy, security and independence. Busy in her mind with things that still need doing, she is now observer and commentator. Born into the last fling of community music, she has lived through its hey-day, decline and revival. Once always out and on the go, this grand old lady of east-Galway-in-exile now rarely plays at sessions, but instead immerses herself in a great collection of memories and music from her home place.

The home of my childhood, into ruins 'tis fallen
The dear ones who loved me shall greet me no more
Yet I think of it still, joyous visions recalling
Tho' the long grass is growing on the step of the door.

FROM 'SWEET INNISCARRA'
(LEARNED BY LUCY FROM PADDY BREEN
IN LONDON IN 1950)

Len Graham
and
Pádraigín Ní Uallacháin

BY FINTAN VALLELY

Little said, soonest mended and a few words are best
And them that speak seldom they are surely blest
I speak from experience, my mind tells me so
If everyone had their own love they'd know where to go.

FROM THE SONG 'GREEN GROWS THE LAUREL'

South Ulster describes a territory that pre-dates annexation and the border. It covers north Monaghan, north Louth and south Armagh. It has a considerable poetic legacy of classical writers from the 1700s, such as Séamas Dall Mac Cuarta, Peadar Ó Doirnín and Art McCooey. McCooey's work indeed has, uniquely, filtered into the local folksong repertoire. Best known is Úr-Chill a Chreagáin, sung for decades to a sentimental version of the air. Into this picture comes Mary Harvessy who had learned this and other songs from a grandmother removed from the poets by only a generation. An enterprising Father Luke Donellan recorded her singing on an Ediphone cylinder around 1918, and this passed to the Folklore Commission in Dublin, where Séamus Ennis learned it. Five generations of technology later, *sean nós* singer Pádraigín Ní Uallacháin has reunited the air to the lyrics and the piece is now central to her repertoire of long-forgotten songs of the area.

She sees herself now as 'a link in a continuous chain; with a duty to make available the songs that had lain dormant'. One move back from her is her Dundalk father Paddy Weldon, a *sean nós* singer himself, who in 1926 had been in the first group brought to learn Irish in the Donegal

Rann na Féirste Gaeltacht. His mentor locally in Louth was song collector and language organiser Larry Murray. Separating Pádraigín from her objective is a formidable obstacle – the death of the Irish language in south Armagh/Louth. 'The language preserved the songs and, once the language went, within the space of thirty years the next generation neither had language nor songs. That's massive in terms of the effect on society.' However, between Murray's written transcriptions and Donellan's recordings, she has great advantage, for they have provided her with words, tonic solfa transcriptions and sometimes the singing. The value of this as a key to music style in earlier times is invaluable. 'Some of the airs are so ancient in their style they don't make sense to any of us who are used to a regular song-form.'

Pádraigín Ní Uallacháin was born in 1950. Her mother was Eithne Devlin from Cullyhanna, County Armagh, in whose father's family Irish still survived. Pádraigín's father had spent his younger years in Rann na Féirste with singers like Máire John and Neilí Mhór. A schools inspector, he was obliged to uproot every few years, and so the family was never settled. By the age of two Pádraigín was in Mayo, Donegal at seven, by thirteen she was at boarding school in Monaghan, at eighteen in Dublin, then to Derry. Now she is finally settled in Mullaghbane, County Armagh. Irish was the language of growing up, and, in an English-speaking world, this intensified her sense of being on the outside. Her brother Ruaidhrí played uilleann

pipes, and her sister Eithne sang and played flute. Pádraigín learned piano. The literature in their home included many song collections.

She was separated from the family for a year at the age of twelve, living with an old couple in the Ros Guill Gaeltacht, and this she feels informs the intensity of song for her today. This helped her get a scholarship to St Louis secondary school in Monaghan. 'Its singing tradition was a great comfort. There was a great emphasis on the choir – everybody was in it. And I remember looking forward to old nuns dying, because it meant you would be preparing for the funeral for three days so you would be singing non-stop. *Dies irae, dies illa!* That was the highlight of my school years.' She took singing lessons with Sister Enda there too, 'just enough to help me with breathing techniques but not enough to ruin my traditional voice'.

She went to college at UCD in 1969, but dropped out. She spent her weekends in Connemara, where she heard Seosamh Ó hÉanai and Máire Áine Nic Dhonncha. She acted in Irish plays in the Damer theatre and a few summers and winters were spent working on Irish Sea ferries before she went back to college to do Irish studies at Coleraine in 1973. After this, she became the first woman to read the news in Irish on RTE television, this overlapping with presenting and researching her own programme for television. 'It was fantastic training and discipline, and gave me an idea of standards in everything I do.' She researched and presented *Reels of Memory* on radio between 1979 and

1981. She then studied for an MA at Coleraine on the Irish song tradition. All this took in a social life that brought her to the Northern Ireland Arts Council's first, heady 1978 Beleek singing weekend and its many offspring, thus re-awakening her own need to sing. She married Antrim singer Len Graham in 1982, and through him spent weekends with the south Donegal fiddlers, and took part in all-night song parties in Sarah Anne O'Neill's in Tyrone and song-swapping at Eddie and Gracie Butcher's of Magilligan, County Derry.

By then they had two children, so she stepped out of the public world of song, learning new material and working out songs of her own, researching and listening. Their move to Mullaghbane, County Armagh, was very positive for her, allowing her to focus on the south Ulster material that interested her. She had a huge collection of songs in Irish which she wanted to make available to others. 'I wanted to do a record of the songs I loved, but also I realised, as a parent and a teacher, that there was no song material on albums for families.' The magnificent children's song collection of thirty-six pieces, *A Stór 's A Stóirín*, was the result in 1994. *An Dara Craiceann* followed as her personal song statement in 1995, and then, for young people, *When I Was Young*, recorded with Len in the English language in 1996. In the same year she organised and produced a CD of songs and music for Gaelscoil Dhún Dealgan, where she teaches.

Len Graham was born in 1944 in Glenarm, in the heart of the Glens of Antrim. But, like Pádraigín's, his family moved around quite a lot, following the fortunes of his journeyman cabinet-maker father and ending up in Belfast — though always retaining a strong sense of belonging in the Glens. Both his parents sang local songs from counties Derry and Antrim: 'But of course I didn't realise till much later that these were folk songs! My earliest recollection was hearing Glenarm mentioned in a song — my grandmother singing "Glenarm Bay".' His mother, Eveline Robinson, was a singer and danced the old sets. 'She and I danced the "Stack of Barley" the day I got married. We were the only two who could dance a schottische!' As a child she had witnessed the last of the Irish speakers in the Glens, and had heard keening women at funerals. She was a cousin of John Rea, the Glens hammer-dulcimer player. Len's father, Samuel, came from a family of fourteen, and because he was considered musical he was bought a fiddle as a child: 'Then the fiddle was handed on to the next down, my uncle Walter, so he made up for it by playing the mouth organ and Jew's harp.' Len remembers him enthusiastically juggling glass batteries and wireless knobs to locate Athlone radio, and playing records of Richard Hayward, Delia Murphy, Kathleen Ferrier and Fritz Kreisler on the gramophone. 'He was a very passionate man and a great singer. He was one of the few singers who made the hair stand on the back of my neck.'

Len's school years were fragmented — three years here,

three years there. At fourteen, a great interest in travelling took him hostelling around Ireland. 'The An Óige youth hostel network was the most liberating experience for a young lad then living in Belfast. I got to know every nook and cranny in Ireland. I met great characters and musicians, and I got a chance to sing out. All I can ever remember was singing. They used gag me with a scout scarf to keep me from singing!'

He left school at fifteen to work in a factory, and by the age of sixteen he was in Belfast. Through An Óige he found his way to Donegal with Johnny and Mickey Doherty, and to Fermanagh with Cathal McConnell. And he heard about *fleadhanna*. 'The first one I got to was Mullingar in '63. I had walked and hitched from Ballymoney in County Antrim. Those early *fleadhanna* were magic — endless sessions and singing. Nobody went to bed!' In 1966 he entered the competitions and came second to Nioclás Tóibín in the English-language song. Remarkable indeed was the difference in pedigree of the songs proffered: 'Nioclás sang the "Dawning of the Day" and I sang "The Moorlough Shore".' Len won it himself in 1971, then hung up his competition gloves with confidence. At that time too he witnessed Willie Clancy playing 'Dark is the Colour' on the pipes in Friel's of Milltown Malbay: 'After hearing him play that air, I just had to get the words!'

At the end of his teens, in 1963, he met singer Joe Holmes at a Derry and Antrim fiddlers' session in Ballymoney, beginning a friendship and a legendary duet that were to last until Joe's death in 1978. 'I started taking Joe to *fleadhs*. And we had dozens of houses where the people were into what we were into.'

Comhaltas started up in Ballycastle in 1966. Its chairman, Frank McCollum, was also the master of the Loyal Orange Lodge, and a collector of tunes and songs. This provided other gatherings for song. Meeting source-singer Eddie Butcher of Magilligan was another great milestone in Len's singing. 'We became friends and that friendship lasted. If I didn't go down to see him every week, there was always a phonecall.'

Everybody of that generation — his father's, Joe's and Eddie's — appeared to have been a singer in Len's estimation: 'I remember seeing sixty or seventy musicians and singers at Derry and Antrim fiddlers sessions and there was nothing unusual about it at all.' There was no visible organisation, no body, and no rules. 'I think they were conscious that things were changing, and somebody reckoned it would be a good idea to keep it going.' Religion was no part of it, as is still the case. 'I was taken to those gatherings as a cub in the 1950s, and I remember my father pointing out "There's a two and a half there, there's a compass there, there's a pioneer pin there, there's a *fáinne* there," and I remember his saying, "Where else would you get this sort of gathering? That's the way it should be."' Later, in the 1960s, Len met the Keanes — Dolores, and her aunts Sarah and Rita of Caherlistrane, Galway — at the Connacht *fleadh* in

Ballinasloe. This generated a great exchange of songs and singers southward for many years and gave Dolores the 'Ramblin' Irishman' for her record with De Danann.

Although never a conscious collector, Len knows the value that his singing and travelling have for preserving and keeping alive this spirit. He recorded an LP with Joe Holmes in 1975, *Chaste Muses, Bards and Sages,* the title taken from the first line of one of Len's songs. Next came the solo, *Wind and Water,* in 1976, then *After Dawning,* with Joe Holmes, in 1978. *Do Me Justice* followed in 1983 and *Ye Lovers All* in 1985. He started the group Skylark with Gerry O'Connor, Garry O'Briain and Andrew McNamara in 1986 and still tours with them sporadically. However, since 1990 he has performed in partnership with Mullaghbane storyteller John Campbell, a combination that mixes serious song with 'likely' tales and which they have brought with great acclaim to schools, festivals and clubs all over these islands and to college campuses in the US.

Len's most treasured collecting project has been the wonderful field-recordings series *Harvest Home,* and, in 1992, recognition for this work gained him the Seán O'Boyle Cultural Traditions Award. He continues, uniquely, as a professional unaccompanied singer. Pádraigín is collaborates on music projects with Danish composer Palle Mikkelborg, harper Helen Davies and piper Liam O'Flynn. She also plans to record an album of exclusively unaccompanied south-Ulster, Irish-language song. She and Len perform together frequently, bilingually and in unison,

and with *port a' bhéals,* and now they are planning an unaccompanied album. In 1997 the Feakle Traditional Singing Festival marked appreciation of this whirl of activity with a joint award for their contribution to the Irish song tradition.

'S dá mbéinnse eolach ar dhéanamh ceoil binn
Ó thriallfainn leatsa amach san oích'
Go gleannta coille amuigh ar an uaignis
Agus cairde dílse bheith linn a choích'.

(If I but knew how to make sweet music
I would follow you into the night
To the wooded glens away together
And loyal friends with us always.)

FROM THE SONG 'A ÓGÁNAIGH ÓIG'

Gary Hastings

BY FINTAN VALLELY

Farewell, you Barney, with the outstretched hand.
Years ago for pleasure as you might understand.
Years ago for pleasure as you might all recall,
When Irishmen throughout the land were brothers one and all.

FROM REPERTOIRE OF EDDIE BUTCHER
AS SUNG BY JACKY DEVENNY

'I used to get approached every so often by RTE and what they want is a "house-trained, Irish-speakin', flute-playin' Northern Protestant". And when they find an Irish-speakin', house-trained, flute-playin' Northern Prod they're highly intrigued and say, "Isn't it wonderful?" you know, or else "Isn't it great to hear *them* playing *our* music?"' So regales Gary Hastings, Church of Ireland rector of the parish of Aughaval in west Mayo. For him, traditional music cannot be annexed by political loyalty, it is the music of the island. In a 1998 Bord Fáilte magazine interview he describes it as an art that mediates material life and spirituality. He may use it to allegorise a theological point – 'It's the same tune, but different, mutated by time and man' – or he will invoke biblical ponderousness to illuminate music's polemics – 'We could sing, long before anyone taught us the words.'

Gary Hastings grew up on the Woodstock Road in east Belfast. From no particular musical background, he learned to play the bagpipes at the age of eleven or twelve. 'The Boys' Brigade had a pipe band and I was in that for a year. I learned "Abide with Me", "Stand up for Jesus" – and a wheen of damned things like that – but only for a year or so, and then I got sense. Puberty arrived and the pipes went out the window!' A child of the music revival, when he did begin to play flute, it was all down to him: 'But it was a help, for when I came to play Irish music you were doing pretty much the same thing – only different. And I knew how to play a whistle, from the pipe chanter, so I learned it brave and fast. Then I got on to the flute, and, I know it's unfashionable to say, but I learned off Chieftains and Bothy Band records.'

Attending university at Coleraine led him off the rails into temptation: 'I went to university to do a degree in physics, and I learned the tin whistle instead. I discovered the world – wee girls and fags and drink – all at the one time!' Ciarán Curran (of Altan) was there at the time, and singers Brian Mullins and Pádraigín Ní Uallacháin. Len Graham was around too, singer Jackie Devenny, and accordionist Ciarán Kelly. Eddie Butcher of Magilligan was alive at the time and Joe Holmes was singing still. 'There was nearly too much music about the place. But it was a great way to learn. Fermanagh hadn't been discovered yet, so I went down there a few times to Séamus Quinn, Mick Hoy [fiddlers], Eddie Duffy [flute] and Jim McGrath [accordion].' Then he visited Fermanagh flute player Cathal McConnell, of the group Boys of the Lough: 'He taught me more in two days than I had learned in the whole of the two years before that – or for ten years after that again. He

showed me things on the flute – what you could do, how you do them, why you wouldn't do them. He was the makings of me, as far as I'm concerned.'

Having thus seen the light, he drifted into playing with the Shaskeen Céilí Band for a while, then decided to do the job properly: 'I went back to do a degree in Irish studies, and part of the thing was a course in folklore.' The next three years continued the storm of sessioning, but in context. Essays required by the course led him into studying the Lambeg drum and fife. This demanded interviewing players and makers, leading him in a full circle back to Antrim flute player John Kennedy, Willie Nicholl and whistle player Willis Patton, 'boys that I knew as good traditional players, but I never knew they fifed and drummed as well!' He collected tunes on these rambles, realising that a good chunk of marching music used the same tunes as dance music, played with a different rhythm. 'I got a hundred and twenty tunes, and only five or six of them were "party" tunes. And two of those were Republican!' He collected 6/8 tunes – but in hornpipe time, reels in hornpipe time as well – all dating to the previous century: 'Things that might have been like Donegal highlands before they were rehashed into fifing time. What it showed me is that Protestants in the early 1800s were playing jigs, reels and hornpipes. That might not seem strange to some people, but the Prods has forgot!'

He experienced the 1960s and the beginning of civil rights agitation as a transition. His parents' generation of

Protestants had attended Clancys concerts in the Kings Hall, but didn't follow through into traditional music because of its identification with 'Irishness' and its revival over the rest of the island. For those Protestants who played, many dropped out over the period of the hunger strikes in 1983–4. 'I was the only Fenian on the Linfield team, as the saying goes. But nobody ever worried about it until that business happened. Suddenly lads felt that there was things that would offend me. I'd only one leg over the fence. I was still going home, so you could get shot awful handy, you know? You can't run with the hare and hunt with the hounds. Suddenly I discovered I was a Prod. Because, up to that, I was just another boy doing Irish music.'

Gary was neither attracted to the music because of its 'Irishness' nor repulsed from it by the political associations of some of its players. His music was played for the *craic*, without agenda or purpose beyond social and aesthetic fulfilment. However, he was always aware that not too far back in the past of Protestant Ulster this was once just the 'popular' indigenous music. Many incidents emphasised this. 'I remember, in a bar in Enniskillen there was a man got up dancing – full, plastered, his legs was plaiting under him! And we were playing tunes and he started to dance and you could see that, though he was falling all over the place, he knew exactly what he was doing. He was late forties. He wasn't doing any stage stuff – he was doing real stuff. I was told he was an Orangeman from such and such a place. I says, "What's he doing that stuff for?" That's when I found

out that the old dances had been preserved in some of the Orange halls, still went on, all the old stuff that had died out everywhere else.'

In his position as rector, he is well aware of antecedents to this dual role of his chronicled by Francis O'Neill in 1913 – Parson Sterling of County Cavan, *c.* 1737, Revd Alex Nicholls of Leitrim, *c.* 1825, Revd Robert Leech of Belturbet, *c.* 1850. But he sees much more in the music than ideology. To his mind the 'gimp' is the important thing, not virtuosity: 'It's dance music. The best players are the ones who can get the right rhythm, and vary it slightly. Or hit it slightly "off" in the right way which emphasises it. There are tunes that have the right rhythm and if you get the right speed on them they just fly for you. They near play themselves.' Playing is also a social thing for him – sessions in Matt Molloy's pub once a week, or more often during the summer. 'The break in between the tunes is the cement that keeps the tunes together. That's what gives it structure and what makes sense of it, more than the actual music itself. The music is part of a bigger thing. The people that give you the tunes and the connections you have with them are what gives them sense. Other than that, they're just a series of notes.'

Gary's playing has a distinctive 'burbling' sound, careful and precise. 'It's just the way I do it. Generally I would be quite a precise kind of man. I've created variations without smothering my intentions. But there are other boys with music just dripping out of them – like Gabriel McArdle.'

85

McArdle is a singer and concertina player from Enniskillen, one of the musicians who, in Gary's book, has been born to it. 'Everybody's a good musician sometimes – even the worst player in the world gets it right some night to play a tune the best. But if somebody is extremely musical, they don't need to think about it much. They have the greater degree than, say, I would. So, my style is so measured because I have to watch what I'm doing to get it right! Some have to work at it and some can just do it.'

He is happy to teach his own children the basics of music, but 'I don't want to give them more than a bit.' He doesn't think that it is any particular advantage for children to learn to read music. 'You didn't learn to write before you learned to speak. You can speak away but still be illiterate.' Musicality, he explains, is a pressure which invades the psyche. Allen Feldman's interview with Teelin (Donegal) fiddler Con Cassidy is his image: 'Con Cassidy said he learned the fiddle at six or seven. And Feldman said, "It must have given you great advantage?" And Con said, "No! That's not the case. No," he says, "there's lots of fellas, and when they're seventeen or eighteen, this kind of red mist comes down over them. And all there is in the world for them is music. And them's the best musicians! Them ones go 'boom!'" That red mist came over me, completely. I had lost all control, everything went out the window except music. And I know other fellas, like Séamus Quinn, and he had the same phenomenon, like everything went out of his head except music. And that is definitely a great thing. You

should still give the child the music basics and then leave them alone – they'll do what they want to do themselves – and if the explosion happens at seventeen, then they'll be fine, they'll have had a wee bit of a start.'

This has been one area of discussion between himself and fiddler Father Séamus Quinn. 'We were chatting one time about it and we have the idea that we were "ordained musicians" rather than "musical priests". Everybody has an identity, and I'm the boy who plays the flute. "Priest" is something that happened to me subsequently. Ordination is an acceptance of self and identity, not a denial of it.'

However, despite the 'social' aspect of the music, he is also aware that musicians rarely ever talk to each other meaningfully. He recalls a night with Dessie Wilkinson in Pat's Bar in Belfast many years ago: 'There was nobody else there, and we didn't feel like playing. We'd known each other about ten years, and he turns around to me and says, "Do you know something – I know bugger all about you." And I says, "I don't know much about you either." So we sat and got quite stewed and found out about each other, and we were great mates after that. Up to that we were just boys who played tunes. You know musicians only in the context of tunes, and so that's why you class them as fiddle players and box players and stuff like that – it's a kind of freemasonry.'

Stardom he sees as nothing new in traditional music. 'We praise them because we want them to be there.' He calls it the 'Johnny Doherty syndrome'. 'I remember being at a session at the Ballyshannon festival. The pub was full of boys — and they were scared to go near him (Doherty). People saw him as "one of the heads; he's on a different level, you know". It's a different class of a thing in our music, you know, but there are boys who are seen as stars.' A star would have to be a good player, in his book, 'but there's also a bit of legend too'.

Gary Hastings might be one of the few traditional musicians to also be a Church of Ireland clergyman, but just as distinctive is the fact that, for a player of his class, he has never made a record. 'I was never asked! Everybody has their way of looking at music and thinking about it, and in sessions you rarely ever get the chance to show what you particularly do, because most people are quite shy. You're only allowed to play so much on your own, if you're with other musicians. But people indulge themselves on LPs. That's a nice thing to do, and I understand why they don't do it in sessions. An LP allows you to say, "Well, this is the way I see things and do things." I like that. That's the only let-out our tradition has. You're not going to stick your head out in our tradition because everybody else would take it off ye, you know. That's just the way it works.'

Martin Hayes

BY FINTAN VALLELY

Playing in the Abbey bar in Chicago one night in 1995, Martin Hayes became aware of a particular group of listeners dressed in dickey bows and tails. They all had fiddle cases. Chatting later, it turned out they were members of the Vienna Philharmonic Orchestra on tour. And they knew what they were listening to. Such an occurrence would have been rare a few decades ago, but today it is a common part of the breaking down of prejudices among music genres. Good music is good music – provided one understands or respects the ground rules. More importantly, a musician with insight can be universally appreciated.

Martin Hayes was born in Feakle, County Clare, in 1962. His father, P. Joe, has been fiddler with the Tulla Céilí Band for fifty years. Profoundly interested from childhood, he was given a half-size fiddle at the age of seven. By twelve he was on to a full-size. 'I just sat and watched my father put his fingers on the fiddle and listened to the tunes.' Since a couple of years before that, he would play records of céilí band music when his parents were out: 'The Tulla, the Kilfenora, old records of Coleman and Morrison, Paddy Cronin. I never missed The Long Note [radio programme] of a Monday night.'

Galligan's bar in Crusheen ran a folk club every Tuesday, and there he saw the greats of Irish music play, including Séamus Ennis. 'I learned a lot of tunes from John Naughton [concertina] from Feakle. He had played the concertina when he was a young fella without really listening to 78s. He had all these old versions of tunes and old ways of playing – what it would have sounded like in reality sixty years ago.' He learned from other local players, including Joe Bane and Bill Malley, Paddy Canny who is his paternal uncle-in-law, and of course from his father. 'I suppose he is the main influence.' P. Joe was an uncompromising teacher: 'not a perfectionist, but like if he didn't think what you played was any good he'd have a very difficult time not telling you so!'

Fiddler Kathleen Collins was a favourite player of his, and Tommy Potts too. Tommy might call in when on one of his visits to Peadar O'Loughlin, Paddy Canny and Seán Reid. 'He'd sit in the middle of the kitchen for the night and just play and pontificate!' P. Joe's playing in the Tulla band was a big part of Martin's life. 'I remember 1969 – on the night Armstrong was landing on the moon – I was sitting on the side of the stage as a child in the middle of the Tulla Céilí Band playing for the Darling Girl from Clare festival.'

Music wasn't taught in the schools he attended, nor played by any of his age group locally. 'By the time I got to my Leaving Cert, I definitely felt marginalised. It was very looked down on, to the point of being ridiculed. I used to be with the Tulla band while most other kids would be watching *Top of the Pops*.' At fourteen he began playing with the band, and by sixteen he was having a life of travel that formal education frustrated. 'I would try and mitch time when the band was going to England. But one time I got on the plane, got off in London, onto the bus to go to the terminal, and who sat down beside me but the principal of the school!' With the band he played *céilí* dances and concerts in all the hallowed spots – the Galtymore, the National, the Irish Centre in Liverpool, the Carousel in Manchester.

A spell of studying business at the National Institute of Higher Education at Limerick overlapped with all this, and the odd *fleadh cheoil* and *Slógadh* competition. He won a junior All-Ireland in Buncrana at fourteen, and a senior a couple of years later. After leaving college, he made wedding videos for a while, then sold frozen TV meals. An ankle injury put him off the road, and so he was tempted to travel to America in 1984 to play in a wedding band. 'I was just drifting. I never thought I could make money playing music; certainly not the music that I liked.'

Earlier trips to America with the Tulla band had brought him in contact with Johnny McGreevy in Chicago, Liz Carroll, Michael Flatley, Séamus Connolly in Boston, and Paddy Cronin. He returned to play a Patrick's Day gig, but wound up on a construction site: 'A lame ankle, owing money to the bank in Tulla, hauling lumber in Chicago – in response to that I drank and partied and had a wild time.' He played in a ballad band: 'It reinforced in me the notion that there was no sense of good taste for music in the world any more, and that there wasn't an audience for it.' He walked off the stage one Patrick's Day and, with Dennis Cahill, formed 'a loud, fast, aggressive rock and roll band,

Irish music on electric fiddle – Midnight Court.' It didn't have much commercial success, but his reputation as a musican helped him survive.

When the band split up and he had done some soul searching, there were friends there to rely on. 'I spent a lot of time playing and running sessions for Tom Looney at the Abbey pub in Chicago. Tom was from north Clare, and his wife Breege became kind of patrons of mine. I was then into the notion of sponsoring and promoting the idea of pure traditional music. I spent most of my day reading books of philosophy and spirituality, meeting people, trying out things, going to the libraries, finding music from all over the world, being sober, being vegetarian.' He was changing everything, but was playing the music he wanted to and living from it. Helen Bommarito, whom he had been close to since the rock days, helped him make a record with Green Linnet, and then he moved to Seattle in 1993.

Since then he comes back touring in Ireland for short spells. He plays what he wants to, as he feels it – and nothing else. 'I wouldn't have a record producer or a record company tell me what to do musically, ever!' But Green Linnet's PR person in Ireland, Amy Garvey, liked the album immensely, and the company promoted it confidently. Tony MacMahon brought him back for a TV show, and he also came over to teach at the Willie Clancy week.

In Chicago he had heard blues and funk jazz, and knew the people of the jazz community and rock and roll scene. He listens to classical music, the Pakistani devotional songs of Nusrat Ali Fateh Khan, Myles Davis. His interest is in the aesthetic of good music and musicianship, which he feels is constantly under attack. 'But it's hard to be a genuine musician today. Commercialism is a terrible drain on you.' The difference between playing music for the love of it and playing it on a stage can be colossal. The musician cannot always be in good form. 'You feel pressure, you feel observed, you feel you must continuously be able to deliver the music and you feel you must be interesting. But it puts pressure on the more easygoing nature of the creative process in music. It's not music of incredible virtuosity, it's music with feeling. And feeling and passion are hard to have all the time.'

He sees the various experiments with Irish music as responding to crises and questions, but he believes that this is now outdated. 'We've been embracing a notion of creative change and innovation that is pushed by commerce.' He believes that music does change, grow and innovate, but 'at a far slower rate than the market can wait for, or people's career needs can deal with. It can't just completely overturn itself every decade.' Martin is hard on himself too, acknowledging that he doesn't always hit the music as he would like to, and makes mistakes: 'It angles at the purity but it doesn't always get there. It's as good as I can do but I'm not in the category of Willie Clancy, Tommy Potts, Pádraig O'Keeffe, Johnny Doherty, Paddy Canny. I'm not of that same level of purity in my music. I'm more compromised. It's like saying that you've read a book about spirituality, but you haven't actually become a monk. Understanding what they have to offer is only the first part; you still have to do the journey.'

Of the living players, he respects fiddler and piper Martin Rochford for being most in touch with what music is about. 'He knows it and is aware of it. He only recognises the aesthetically beautiful in music.' He feels similarly about Junior Crehan, Micho Russell, John Kelly and Pádraig O'Keeffe. 'It's like an ancient, tribal wisdom that was contained, that you couldn't understand. And these fellas actually somehow had carried it from the past – more representatively than O'Neill's book or 78 records.'

One of Martin's mother Peggy's sisters was married to the late Joe Mac who played with the Tulla, another is married to Abbey (Galway) flute player Willie Conroy. Her brother's children John and Séamus MacMahon play in the group Fisher Street. Martin sees music as 'not so much a matter of genes, but of circumstance, exposure, environment, opportunity, encouragement and belief'. He believes that it is easiest to be creative 'inside the body of music that you know. To single out aspects of music based on regionality is an unmusical idea.'

He has no time for music snobbery. 'The fiddle style in classical music is one of a multitude of fiddle styles and cannot be regarded as anything other than that.' He realises that there are crises in all forms of music, old hegemonies collapsing, yet he does not see that traditional music is in any danger of suffocation by popularisation: 'The world was flooded with nonsense at the same time as Bach.' Like anything else, classical music contains within it a lot of nonsense too. There's a lot of Irish music that's a 'mindless muddling through the tunes', but if it isn't there, there's nothing to rise above.

Martin feels that modern education trounces the aesthetic and the sense of reality that music hints at, that no music is just about learning notes. 'The jazz of the fifties – John Coltraine – was spirited, experimental, vibrant. It was alive – and jazz music was outside the system. It was invited in later, and now most university departments of music have almost an equal split between classical and jazz. In jazz right now there's a bunch of people coming out who know everything that Coltraine did. In a sense, they can play as well as any of them – and mean absolutely nothing. You can play somebody's music, but it will not be the same or as good, unless you do an equal journey.'

The intangible aesthetic that he strives for has nothing to do with ornament, tune or repertoire; it is frustrated by the 'burden to be innovative, new, creative'. And the burden to be 'traditional' he finds even bigger. 'Inside the music is a great feeling of insecurity and doubt about its real quality. The feeling is that, if you actually embrace the entire universe of music on equal terms, it might prove to you that what you cherish so dearly may not be truly of the value you believe, and you'd have to risk throwing it all away; which nobody wants to do.'

In his albums he likes to stick to one mood. 'Where

some people make an album with fifteen different moods, I'd make fifteen different albums.'

He likes U2's earlier music, but feels they are now being driven by their empire yet are expected to be creative as well. He toys with the idea that creative people may have just one statement to make in their lives: 'Tommy Potts had one statement all his life.' Likewise he has studied Marc Chagall's painting. At a full exhibition in Chicago, a slice through the painter's life's work, Martin realised that 'the man was literally painting the one painting all his life. His last stuff was actually a coalescing of all he'd ever done.'

Martin Hayes's performance technique is to begin a piece slowly, simply, and then develop it. The tune is the scaffolding, not the skeleton. By means of it is constructed a sensory structure in stylistic, melodic and dynamic variation. The listener is drawn into the mind of the musician and with him supports the illusion. 'I want to make the tune as clear as possible. My playing is a manipulation of the tune for myself and the listener. I probably have an aspect of what the composer intended, but there are shadings in it that will be more attractive to me. I'd take them and mould them into something that speaks for me.'

Peter Horan

BY CHARLIE PIGGOTT

To ask directions in the Irish countryside can sometimes be an interesting experience. Once, in the late 1970s, while making my way from Dublin to a country session, I approached an old man of some eighty years for directions to Ballaghaderreen. 'Ah,' he said, 'it's about nine or eighteen miles up the road!' I've often thought about it since and reckon the odd reply may be connected with the loose expression we sometimes use, 'a mile or two away' – the latter being twice the former.

At any rate, I duly arrived at my destination (nine miles distant) and joined in a great evening's session of music: Paddy O'Brien, the Offaly accordion player, was there with fiddle player James Kelly and several others whose names, like many of the tunes we played, I cannot remember. But the two musicians who presided over the music making that day were Peter Horan and Fred Finn (flute and fiddle), playing with that inimitable native Sligo style characterised by wonderful flexibility, rhythm and lift.

Peter and Fred hail from the Kilavil region of Sligo, in what is known as Coleman country. Though they had played music together for many years, mainly at country house-dances, it wasn't until 1959, when Ciarán Mac Mathúna visited south Sligo to record for his radio programme, *The Job of Journeywork*, that the now famous duet partnership was reinforced. They have given us some great tunes – 'The Kilavil Jig', 'The Humors of Ballyconnell' and 'Fred Finn's Reel' – and enthralled listeners with their music for a period of 25 years, until Fred Finn's untimely death in 1986.

Peter Horan was born in Buninadden, County Sligo, on 25 June 1926. His mother, Margaret Horan (née Davey), was an excellent fiddle player (she also played melodeon and concertina) and Peter mentions that 'she had nice clear open playing'. His father was a good traditional singer but did not play music. Jimmy McGetterick, an old-time tin whistle player from Ballymote, remembered that, around 1930, he heard two women playing fiddles in an old schoolhouse (one was Nora O'Gara and the other Margaret Horan) and he said that, while listening to the excellent music, the fiddles hummed an internal rhythm which he never heard before nor since. Peter clearly remembers playing reels on a tin whistle when just four years old and 'in winter time, at night, when the local people came in, we used to dance those sets that time, and my mother would be playing away for them and I'd be with my little tin whistle and belting away after them . . . that's how I got it'. He soon graduated to fiddle and flute and at fifteen years 'was as good at reel playing on the flute as I am today'.

The number of fine musicians who have sprung from the borders around Ballymote, Gurteen and Kilavil is astonishing and the impact on Irish traditional music by several of these — Michael Coleman, James Morrison and Paddy Kiloran, who emigrated to New York early this century — cannot be overestimated. Through their recordings, these exponents of the jaunty Sligo style came to be widely known and admired. Many more, equally versatile Sligo players, who recorded to a lesser extent or did not record at all, also contributed greatly: Philip O'Beirne, Jim Morrison, Lad O'Beirne, Martin Whynne, Paddy Sweeney and John Joe Gardiner. Others, like John Egan, Kathleen Harrington and Roger Sherlock, introduced this music to Dublin and London.

Peter Horan grew up steeped in this rich tradition of music. Many of the reels popularised by Michael Coleman — 'Lord Gordon's Reel' and 'The Boys of the Lough', often played by Peter's mother Margaret — were ever part of the local Kilavil repertoire and returned polished, as Peter would say, on the new 78 records. Michael Coleman learned much of his music from Lad O'Beirne's father, Philip, a noted fiddler, and his brother Jim Coleman, though never recorded, was reputed to be as gifted as his famous brother. According to Peter's mother, Jim Coleman was the greatest fiddle player of all time. He was also a shy, sensitive man who, it is reputed, developed a life-long fear of darkness after experiencing the *foirdin mara* (death of the senses) and the fairies in his youth. Peter recalls that: ''twas in the ass and cart they used to travel and, if there was a bit of a rambling house, they'd be afraid at night time — ghost stories, this, that and the other. I was listening to them myself, but I drowned them with the music. I forgot about the ghosts when I started playing. But Jim would be travelling on the road. He had no company on the cart and he'd put a hen in a bag and the next thing, if he was passing near an ol' lonesome spot, he'd put his hand over and — cackle, cackle — he was happy then. He had the company, you see.'

As in other parts of Ireland, during the 1930s and 1940s, the tradition of country house-dances gave way to commercial dancing and, with the introduction of *fleadhanna cheoil* by Comhaltas Ceoltóirí Éireann in the 1950s, many new *céilí* bands appeared. In Peter's area the Glenview Céilí Band was set up, composed of local Kilavil musicians: 'Willie Coleman, Fred Finn, Dick Brennan and myself on four fiddles; there was Mick Kelly and Dan Healy, two flutes; Joe and Jerry Fallon, two brothers on two accordions; Paddy Kilmartin, one of the best drummers I think ever stood behind any band — a drummer means an awful lot; and Eileen McDonnell from Knockbow was on piano — lovely piano player — the vamp with music makes or breaks it; it brings you with it, you know.'

Peter also performed with the Coleman Country Céilí Band for several years, which included the renowned flute players Séamus Tansey and Peg McGrath, and with the Martin Whynne *céilí* group.

The world of traditional music can be likened to an extended family: each musician becoming aware of the others' faults and failings, likes and dislikes, and styles, good and bad. Peter says, 'I enjoyed the music and I enjoyed meeting all those people, and I think I've met most of them' — Joe Burke, the Lennons of Kiltyclogher, Fermanagh-born Séamus Quinn and fiddle player Seán Maguire. In conversation, names float naturally to the surface, not unlike the flow of his own fine music.

He speaks in glowing terms of the fiddle music of Father Séamus Quinn, who has adopted and adapted the Coleman style of playing. 'I met him once below in Antrim for a weekend playing for Cavan set dancers. Father Séamus Quinn was the most powerful fiddle player . . . and Cavan had a great set dancing group that time. If you heard the music that came out of that fiddle! I don't know what kind of fiddle he had, because no strings would ever stand the power that he was putting through it. Well, the Lord save us, he'd drown fifty musicians — power, strength and power — and 'twas all there for the dancers, he jumping them up to the roof, you know.'

Peter feels that the best flute music he ever performed was in Tobercurry in duet session with the noted Seán Maguire. He has the greatest respect for Seán Maguire's fiddle playing and reckons that 'when Maguire wanted to settle playing music, there's none of them would touch him'.

However, one musician whom he praises with a special reverence is his boyhood friend, Martin Whynne. 'Martin was a gentleman, a brilliant man and a beautiful fiddle player. He played just as it came to him, nice and easy. He had a sweet bow-hand and when he would play they'd leave down the fiddles to listen to him.' The two musicians grew up together around Buninadden, where Martin was born in 1916. In the early 1940s he emigrated to London and in

1948 to New York City to join his fellow Sligo musicians there. New York has been his home ever since. A great musician and composer, with some six or seven compositions to his credit, he rated Lad O'Beirne among his own favourite players.

Although Peter's and Martin Whynne's paths hadn't crossed for many years, an occasion did present itself in 1972 when the Coleman Country Céilí Band were invited to the US. Having performed in several cities, including Boston and Chicago, the band concluded its tour with a farewell reunion and celebration of Sligo fiddle music in John O'Donnell's Hall, New York city. For Peter it was an unforgettable and emotional experience. 'All the lads were there – Lad O'Beirne, Andy McGann, Paddy Reynolds, Larry Redican, Mulhaire, the whole bunch of them – and poor old Martin Whynne never came in; he was in the outer bar.' Due to his shy and retiring nature, Martin had ceased session playing many years previously.

Peter reminisces about his blunt determination to entice his friend on stage for the finale:

And I remember
I had such love for Martin Whynne
They were all there crying
Poor ol' Lad O'Beirne was crying on stage
He was delighted to meet people from his own area, you know.
But to make a long story short anyway.
The National Anthem was called

And Alfie Dineen was the leader of the band and he says
We'll all stand up.

I said to Alfie, listen, says I, Alfie,
There's one man I want here
Martin Whynne, I said
There're all here, but my best friend is Martin Whynne
You know, blunt as that.
So we waited and he called Martin Whynne. No come.
And when you wait like that, a second is like five minutes.
But anyway I said give him another call
And he announced it on the mike.
Martin Whynne is needed at the stage. No reply again.
And says I, I'm in trouble now surely.
Well says I, third time lucky and begod he did
And all the people stood up
Well I was that determined that I wanted him there
And that was the whole team.

Here he comes and I handed him the fiddle
And I stood up beside him
And we played the National Anthem.
I never will forget that, poor old fella.

Martin visited Ireland in 1989 and was made honorary president of the All-Ireland *fleadh cheoil* in his native Sligo, in recognition of his contribution to traditional music, and he teamed up again for some fine duet music with his friend Peter Horan.

Peter has taken his long musical life in his stride — teaching, performing, recording, adjudicating, touring and broadcasting on radio and television. He attracted attention some years ago on television when asked to comment on Seán Ó Riada's now classic blending of traditional music with classical music. 'I've the greatest respect for Seán Ó Riada and his work, but the day you modernise Irish traditional music is the day you kill it,' was his reply.

Peter confines his musical talents to flute and fiddle, on which he is master of the Coleman style. He was also, he says, a fine singer: 'I'd a lovely tenor voice at fourteen years of age and could have been in America. I used to sing all John McCormack's songs.' Seemingly, a returned Yank wished to take him back to New York to have his voice trained, but his mother insisted he remain on home turf. 'I never regretted it. I stayed with the old music and the *craic*. People would be thinking through the years, well I'm sorry I didn't do it when I got the opening. I mightn't have got an opening, it could be the closing. I stayed in the home place.'

Friends, relations and admirers of his music are grateful he did not emigrate. Peter Horan is now the last of his kind; at 72 years of age he is still music making and can be regularly heard playing great favourites like 'Farewell to Erin' and 'The Maid in the Cherry Tree'. His old friend Martin Whynne died recently and Peter is 'the only one left holding Sligo music around his native Kilavil'.

It has often been said by older exponents that traditional music must be played purely for love. Love should take precedence over all and only then do the tunes come out in their glory. Listen to Cooley's music. He caressed the tunes with loving care and they have endured. Peter's final comment is that 'we know now what's happening music. There's a mint of money made on music now but I wouldn't care about it. I loved it and I wouldn't care if I never made a penny. I worked for my living but I still played my music.' Fair play to him!

Returning home from a recent session in Rossinver, County Leitrim, with Peter and fiddle player Ben Lennon, we skirted the town of Gurteen ('the small meadow'). This reminded me of the night I met a man in Gort Inse Guaire ('the island meadow of Guaire') who met a Yank who asked how far he was from Galway city. 'As the crow flies, it's about fifteen miles,' came the reply. 'I know,' said the Yank, 'but if the goddamn crow was on a bicycle, how far would it be?' I like to think that he stumbled on a good session of music.

Tommy Keane
and
Jacqueline McCarthy

BY CHARLIE PIGGOTT

Mention of Irish traditional music calls to mind counties like Clare, Kerry, Galway, Sligo and Donegal. However, the important contribution made by Wicklow, Wexford and Waterford to Irish piping is well documented. Families of musicians including the Cashes, Dorans, Rowsomes and Pottses originated here. The fiddle playing of Tommy Potts has been influential not least in areas like east Clare and the piping of Leo Rowsome has had a marked effect on many young players. One of the most famous and colourful characters in traditional music, the travelling piper Johnny Doran, had his roots in the south-east and was responsible for introducing the Milltown Malbay player, Willie Clancy, to the art of piping. The tradition in this region is maintained today by the present generation of young pipers, among them Jimmy O'Brien-Moran and Tommy Keane.

Tommy Keane was born in Waterford city in 1953. Although his immediate family did not play traditional music, he learned the rudiments of whistle playing while attending school. Encouragement towards a career in piping came from local piper Tommy Kearney, who in turn received his instruction from another noted Waterford piper, Liam Walsh. Tommy Kearney's musical life is interesting in view of the fact that his initiation into piping arose from a misunderstanding. As a child he often sheltered on rainy days in the house of John Henebry, an uilleann pipe maker who possessed a large number of wax cylinder recordings featuring some of the finest piping of the time. The pipe maker was under the illusion that the young Kearney showed a keen interest in piping, as he passed the time listening to these recordings, whereas he simply could not play outside due to prevailing weather conditions. He subsequently took up piping only to please Henebry.

This sequence of events would later seal Tommy Keane's fate as a piper. Fiddle player John Dwyer, who lived in the Waterford area, was also a major inspiration. A garda sergeant by profession, he was also a member of a renowned musical family from Béara in west Cork who were noted for their many fine compositions, such as 'The Crosses of Annagh' and 'The Holly Bush'.

Tommy emigrated to London in 1980 and soon joined the traditional music scene there, which included players like Tommy McCarthy, Bobby Casey, Brendan Mulkere and John Bowe. It is often said that immigrant performers express themselves through their music. Many young players, like Tommy Keane at this time, had a distinct advantage over musicians at home in that they found themselves in the company of instrumentalists from all over Ireland; tunes, technical skills and styles from other counties were therefore more accessible to them. Tommy's lively interest in piping led to involvement with the newly formed Pipers' Club in the city. 'The Sense of Ireland festival had been on just before I went over. And one of the things that came out of it was that Na Píobairí Uilleann had a special pipes section and were running piping concerts and had a display of old photographs. A couple of London pipers, including Tommy McCarthy and another Waterford piper, Billy Browne, decided it would be a good idea to set up a pipers' club in London. So I ended up teaching there every Thursday night. It's still going strong now.'

Na Píobairí Uilleann, founded in 1968, provides a platform whereby Irish pipers can come together at an annual *tionól* or gathering. 'The first one I went to was in 1972. 'Twas in Termonfeckin, County Meath, and you'd have seventy or eighty pipers there for a weekend. So that was a fantastic baptism, if you like. You'd be coming away and your head would be swimming with the sound of pipes, you know. So I just missed meeting the likes of Leo Rowsome and Willie Clancy. But, fortunately, I heard Séamus Ennis a good few times.'

Due to a renewed interest in Irish piping in recent years, many clubs were formed in countries like America, Holland and New Zealand, and in Germany regional gatherings are not uncommon. Tommy Keane now devotes much of his musical energies to teaching and is often invited abroad to perform and demonstrate piping techniques. He recalls a musical encounter with Séamus Ennis from his own novice years in Milltown Malbay while practising a reel he had learned called 'The Sailor's Bonnet'.

'I was playing away with my head down and next thing I looked up and here was Ennis coming down the stairs and walking over to me. He told me that I was playing it all right but that there was something maybe in the second part. Well, he came over, knelt down on one knee, turned the chanter around and put it on his knee. I still had the bag and bellows strapped on and was pumping away and he played it through a couple of times and looked up at me, had I got it type of thing, you know. And he just said: "That's more like piping, isn't it!"'

During Tommy Keane's seven-year stay in London he often performed in the famed White Hart in Fulham Broadway and in the Good Mixer in Camden Town. He was in constant demand as a session musician and contributed recordings to many albums while in the city. When the National Theatre Company staged a play called *The Romans in Britain*, he was called upon to provide music for the production. Return journeys to Ireland were a common occurrence for many London musicians and on two occasions he and his fellow musicians, collectively known as the Thatch Céilí Band, won the All-Ireland senior *céilí* band competition. The band consisted of Roger Sherlock and Paul Gallagher (flutes), Adrian Burke, Bobby Casey and Brendan Mulkere (fiddles), Mick O'Connor (banjo), John Bowe (accordion), Tommy Keane (pipes), Kevin Taylor (piano) and Mick Whelan (drums). The name derives from the Thatch pub run by drummer Mick Whelan. Many of these popular Irish venues have long since disappeared, and are now only a distant treasured memory for many traditional musicians: among them the Bedford, frequented by Maggie Barry and Michael Gorman, Con Curtin's

Balloon and the Shakespeare on Holloway Road where Roger Sherlock and Kit O'Connor often played. I'm told that the site of one venue, the Whickey Whackey in Stonebridge Road, is now claimed by a parish church. During the official opening of the blessed building, one of the pub's clientele informed the padre that consecration of the ground would not be necessary as it had been well consecrated over the years!

The involvement of Britain in the Second World War created conditions for massive employment. Farm workers who had signed up for service needed to be replaced and, in the 1950s, many Irish were employed in the construction industry. One of the many emigrant musicians to gravitate to London at this time was piper and concertina player Tommy McCarthy from Kilmihill, County Clare. His offspring would all eventually become musically proficient and, in 1987, his eldest daughter Jacqueline married piper Tommy Keane, creating the pipes/concertina combination we know today.

Jacqueline doesn't ever remember having formal lessons but 'absorbed the music' from the London music scene she experienced at first hand: the playing of Máirtín Byrnes, Paddy Taylor, Bobby Casey and Jimmy Power. 'There was always music in the house, with musicians passing through London.' Traditional music was at its zenith in the capital throughout the 1950s and 1960s, and musicians were in constant demand to perform at functions for the large Irish communities around Kilburn, Camden Town and Shepherd's Bush.

'There was the Irish Centre in Camden Town. There used to be a Comhaltas session there every Monday night and if you weren't in by eight o'clock you wouldn't get a seat. It was packed and really thriving. That would be in the late sixties, with people like Raymond Roland, Finbarr Dwyer and Liam Farrell always there. We used to have Irish dancing, you see, downstairs — we were all still at school then. And we'd go up afterwards, up to this session. Then we had a gig in the Irish Centre on a Sunday morning as a family, for about six years. Different people passing through London would drop in and there would be a lot of Connemara people there, like the *sean nós* singer Treasa Ní Mhiolláin. So we would have been exposed to *sean nós* dancing and *sean nós* singing. That's why, to this day, I love Connemara dancing and singing.'

An eagerly awaited event in the McCarthy family calendar was the annual trip to Ireland. 'We'd get on the boat and the first stop would be John Kelly's in Capel Street. My father would run in and say, "I'll be back in a minute." Three hours later we'd be still in the car. Or we'd go in to play in the Four Seasons or to visit the McKennas in Thomas Street. And then we'd head west. In those days people used to think we were weird playing Irish music. 'Twasn't the done thing. So we never really felt we were at home until we arrived in Milltown Malbay, in to Maisie Friel's. It wasn't like going to a pub — it was just like going into someone's kitchen because it was quiet and Willie Clancy would be there and Séamus Ennis was there the odd time, real characters. We used go there every year.'

These annual visits provided contact with other musicians and regular trips to *fleadhanna* were not uncommon. Jacqueline remembers on one occasion travelling to the All-Ireland *fleadh cheoil* in Listowel with Máirtín Byrnes, P. J. Crotty and Angela Crehan and Willie Clancy; having visited the legendary Mrs Crotty's pub in Kilrush *en route*, numerous sets were danced during the Shannon ferry-crossing.

Her father's friend John Kelly, noted for his gutsy west-Clare style of concertina playing, ranks among her favourite performers. Growing up in London, Jacqueline was under the illusion that most people in Ireland or at least in County Clare had a knowledge of traditional music. 'I thought everyone played music or knew of music or was interested. I just had this image, because every time we came over we always played music. But I remember, when Tommy Peoples's first record was released in the early seventies, I went into a shop and asked for the record and they'd never heard of it. I think that was one of the biggest shocks of my life.'

The McCarthy family can be heard making music regularly together. Jacqueline is also a member of the Sergeant Early Band, which performs traditional music for a contemporary ballet production, *Sergeant Early's Dream*, by the London-based Rambert Dance Company, an association which goes back to 1984 and has taken her to Poland, Egypt and Greece. She now resides in Galway, where she teaches traditional music with her piper husband Tommy Keane and still plays the same Wheatstone concertina purchased in London when she was just nine years old. The pipes/concertina combination works well, Tommy's uilleann pipes being fitted with toned-down reeds, producing his characteristic mellow piping. Like many present-day pipers, his style combines legato and staccato piping, an influence derived from several older players.

Tommy and Jacqueline's musical repertoire includes many old tunes, like 'The Gallowglass', 'Snow on the Hills', 'The Maid at the Well' and 'Eileen Curran'. As a duet partnership, they represent a younger generation steadfastly holding to the tradition in Ireland.

BLOOMING MEADOWS

Paddy Keenan

BY FINTAN VALLELY

Jeremy Marre's 1985 BBC series, *Beats of the Heart*, detailed the origins, movement and culture of the northern hemisphere's 'Roma' (Romany peoples). Central to survival in their two-thousand-year migration from India was music, and preserving the integrity within that was both the Roma's strength of identity and the land-locked people's rejection of them as 'outsiders'. No stronger this than among Ireland's 'Travellers' — Pavees, tinkers, gypsies — who, until the turn of this century, by virtue of travelling from community to community, were established as the supreme transmission and survival mechanism of what we know now as 'traditional' music. Central to that image is the piper, and best known of these in the memories of many of our present-day musicians were the Cashes and Dorans, their technical skills and repertoire by now well absorbed into settled people's notion of 'Irish' music.

An unforgivable racism, lack of understanding and intolerance all run parallel with settled Irish folks' romanticism about and recognition of nomadic people's cultural integrity. However, despite this, identification with the music still thrives within our variously settled, semi-settled and still travelling Pavee people. For the brilliance associated with piper Johnny Doran or fiddler John Doherty neither came easier to them nor was any less dependent on musical genius than among those who learned music in any other class or spectrum of Irish culture. Music may well be 'passed on', but skills have always had to be learned, and there were few tougher

107

teachers and more rigorous adherents to standards than John Keenan of Ballyfermot who died back in 1992.

Growing up in Longford and Westmeath, he was a talented multi-instrumentalist on flute, banjo and pipes whose father also played mainly flute, but also pipes. His wife, Mary Bravender, who played banjo and accordion, came from Cavan town and had an ancestor of German or Austrian extraction; her father was a stationmaster and played fife in a local band. The couple originally travelled for several years. However, they had six children and Mary wanted an education for them, and so in 1955 they moved into a Corporation house in the new Ballyfermot area in Dublin. John continued to work at what today would be classed as 'recycling' – scrap collection with horse and cart. Down the street lived fiddler Ted Furey, father of Finbar, with whom John had a close relationship, the pair spending a lot of recreational time together fishing, playing music and busking. The eldest of the Keenan children was Johnny, then came Eileen, Paddy, Tommy, Brendan and Angela.

Music was an important part of their lives, John playing a half-set of uilleann pipes both for recreation and in pubs. He taught young Johnny, who in turn, in about 1958, taught Paddy the whistle. All the children play, though not all of them professionally. Drawn to the pipes, a couple of years after starting whistle Paddy picked up his father's instrument and played 'Rakish Paddy'. From then on he was designated as 'the piper' in the family. He was bought a Matt Kiernan practice set, by the age of ten or

eleven had a full John Clarke set, and, at the age of twelve, in 1962, he was given a new Rowsome set – the chanter of which he still plays.

In 1961 Ted Furey had given Finbar a set of Kennedy pipes and, when adolescent–parent tensions led to the son residing with the Keenans, there followed five years of sessioning that was often witnessed by the milkman. This earned the Keenan house the nickname 'Radio One, sixteen Oranmore Road' – all this, and with school too often following the 'big nights'. A strict disciplinarian, rigorous perfectionist and believer in the supremacy of technique, John Keenan taught Finbar Furey the pipes too, but – to allow them space for individuality – took them separately. Finbar stayed with the Keenans for five years berore leaving Ireland in 1966. John Keenan drove Finbar and his brother Eddie to the ferry for Scotland on that occasion – the Fureys' first step on their route to music history.

During this period the flamboyant travelling piper Felix Doran, winner of three Oireachtas competitions and almost a legend, was a visitor to the Keenans. He was deeply impressed by Paddy's playing, hearing in it the style of his brother Johnny Doran, and wanted Paddy to join him and son Michael (also a piper) in England. Parental insistence kept the fourteen-year-old Paddy at home, however.

His first big gig was at the Gaiety at a Travellers' benefit, this followed by a week of music with actor John Molloy at the Irish Life Theatre. But Paddy and Johnny had been busking from the age of nine, 'to put bread on the table', as Paddy puts it, and later – like their father and Ted Furey – regularly 'doing the football matches'. Johnny and Paddy then teamed up with singer Liam Weldon and singer/guitarist Johnny Flood in 1966 to form a band to play clubs like The Swamp (a movable feast, it was held in Rathmines, Inchicore or anywhere else). They were eventually joined by father John on pipes and mandolin, who – 'as all fathers tend to do!' – took over, running them as The Pavees Club. This became an institution of the 1960s revival, playing Mondays and Tuesdays in Slattery's of Capel Street. Paddy Moloney (of the Chieftains) played there as a guest, so too did Matt Molloy and many others. 'There could be a handful there one week, a football team the next,' says Paddy.

By the age of 17, Paddy had become interested in the blues and guitar, and he crossed back and forth to London – 'living the hippie life' – busking and practically giving up traditional playing altogether for three years. In 1971 he played with a busking skiffle band – The Blacksmiths – and they recorded an album through EMI. A solo album followed for Paddy with Gael Linn, and he was a stand-in for Peter Browne in the group Monroe with Mícheál Ó Domhnaill and Mick Hanly. Playing gigs with Tony MacMahon, Paddy Glacken and Tríona Ní Dhómhnaill led to Seachtar being formed, which later became The Bothy Band, with Matt Molloy, Tommy Peoples and Donal Lunny.

'The Bothies' lasted four years only. Paddy made an album with Paddy Glacken in 1979, and another with Arty McGlynn in 1982. He spent time in Brittany, lived out of the limelight in Clonakilty doing engineering and furniture restoration courses, and selling antiques. He toured in the US in 1991 and has been based there since 1992, playing festivals and the folk circuit coffee-houses.

Johnny, Tommy and Brendan Keenan are the family's other better-known players. Brendan has recorded a solo pipes album, Johnny is shy of the commercial world, Tommy busks and plays gigs. Eileen's daughter plays classical music, her son John plays banjo and whistle, and her other son Pio plays whistle. Angela's son is studying classical music, Johnny's son writes and plays contemporary rock music in the US. Paddy's daughter Marjolaine plays uilleann pipes, his son Éimhín plays whistle.

Davy Spillane cites John Keenan as an important influence, and, certainly for the Keenan family, his strictness has left all of them with music. 'Music was all that my father had to give. He passed on to us the only thing he had to pass on. And he was right, in a sense – music breaks down all language barriers. He knew we would never starve,' says Paddy. The ultimate tribute to that typically paternal mixture of severity and dedication, maternal love and persistence is 'Johnny's Tune, For the Avalon', an air to his father's memory on Paddy's 1996 album. His sisters never played professionally: 'They see the pain and suffering that the brothers have gone through with music.' His mother no longer plays, but 'she listens to the music. She loves it. She probably knows it a lot better than a lot of people who play it – she's been listening to it for so long.'

Born in Trim, County Meath, Paddy may have been parentally obliged to learn to play music, in the same way that many young people are brought into third-level education, but he is not bitter about his father's insistence. 'That was the way with that generation – it was "you'll do this, you'll do that". I didn't like that side of it and that's why, at the age of seventeen, I gave it up for a few years.' He would like his own children to love the music and to play, but feels that 'if you play it, and it's in the family, kids will like it. If they go for it, then help them, but don't force anything on them. Whatever they do, I hope that they're happy and successful.'

The commercial traditional music scene in America isn't the same as it used to be, particularly for soloists. 'New-age' popularity for Irish music is compromising, and often leads performers into fusions, collaborations and instrumentation that they might not otherwise choose. '"Celtic" has become a huge word out here,' says Paddy, 'and it doesn't mean anything. Most instrumentalists – and even the piping – have gone in that direction, because that's where the money is.' When the fashion changes, the record companies will run, but, whether they do or they don't, he knows that it wasn't for them that he started. 'The nice thing about traditional music is that it will never die. But I'd like to think that, if I was to do something commercial with my music, at least if you were to listen in it would be interesting. I love the traditional music, and I love to see new ideas in it, but not gratuitous.' Living around in the US he sees 'a lot of young musicians coming from Ireland, keeping the tradition up. But if they want to play with a band here they have to go commercial – traditional, contemporary, world or new-age.'

Indeed he plans to put a band together to play his own material, but is impatient with the trial and error that this usually involves. He knows the sound he wants to achieve, favouring blends of fiddle, pipes, percussion, congas, guitar, vocals and fiddle. 'Way back to the old days I always wanted The Bothies to do something original, do their own stuff – and of course there was so much talent there – but they didn't. Then Christy [Moore] and Donal [Lunny] had this idea about Moving Hearts, but I wasn't really ready to go three, four, or five years with a band and not be sure if I was going to have anything from it in the end.'

Paddy Keenan is a strong individual, with a definite idea of what he wants in music. He might not always have stuck to the older music in sessions ('How Much is that Doggie in the Window' is one of his party-pieces), but, 'If I played something not traditional – well it was kind of poking at them a bit, and I can see that now – and they came and spoke to me about it. I began to call them the Ssshushiúins at the time! You can't expect to take people into a club and to have them sit quiet. Nowadays some people even from the Bothy Band days come to me and say

"You're losing the roots of the music." Believe me, it was a lot more traditional than those people who asked me!'

He still often meets up with Finbar Furey in Boston. 'Every chance, we meet. There's never enough time to go over the amount of stuff we need to talk about from the sixties.' He no longer bothers with sessions, saving his energy instead for concerts. 'When I do a concert here now I'm guaranteed a crowd, because I'm not seen for nothing in pubs!' He is suspicious of teaching, but only because it can give people information that they are not ready or emotionally equipped to handle properly. 'I used to do it at the Willie Clancy school, and I had all these kids coming down to me afterwards destroying a tune with all that technical stuff that they asked me for. I didn't want to hear kids destroying tunes like that. That stuff is OK when it comes from the mood of the person that's all their lives at it and decides to do it.'

These days he is re-analysing his playing – listening to old recordings – 'and I'm finding that I'm flying a bit, that my rhythm's gone astray. My soul and heart hasn't been in it and I've been losing that side of it. So I'm going back to my roots. Music is a mood and it doesn't matter to me if it's a piece of punk or a piece of classical or whatever.' He also plays saxophone, guitar and accordion and can scratch a tune on the fiddle too. Now in Cambridge, Massachusetts, Paddy Keenan communicates by e-mail and has a page on the Web. He is planning to get a place back home, but for the moment is happy to enjoy what America is giving him.

Ben Lennon

BY CHARLIE PIGGOTT

Although I grew up associated with music from the Kerry tradition – slides and polkas from around Caragh Lake and the fife-and-drum music of Dingle – my introduction to mainstream session playing dominated by jigs, reels and hornpipes did not occur until the late sixties. Those were the days of the folk revival, when country house-music had shifted to the public house.

I can remember two musicians in particular who were responsible for directing my interest to group session playing. One was banjo player Christy Dunne, whose resident pitch at the time coloured Cork city's main thoroughfare along Patrick Street. He played traditional music as fine as I've heard since, and his rendering of great reels like 'Bunker Hill' and 'George White's Favourite' left a treasured lingering magic. The other was the north Leitrim fiddle player, Ben Lennon. If ever there was a grand gentleman of Irish traditional music, the honour should be his. Traditional musicians everywhere instantly recognise the stooped posture, his fiddle grasped under his chin, intent on serious business. There is something philosophical, almost Zen-like, about his approach to music. The oft-quoted comment, 'the world's in a grain of sand', is applicable here: when Ben Lennon settles into a tune, the whole melody appears to reside in the first series of notes. Attention to phrasing and the setting of rhythm and timing has an immediate urgency, aided by the percussive stomp of the right foot in unison with a driven, determined bow-hand.

I first played music with Ben Lennon in the Country Club in Montenotte in Cork city, which hosted a great session for several years in the early 1970s. Ben led this session, along with Sligo fiddler Mick Milne, who travelled the thirty-odd miles each Friday night from west Cork. There was a core gathering of musicians: Dick Tobin, Donal Martin, Matt Teehan, Dick Nangle and Lena Bean Uí Shé, who sang a great version of 'Mary on the Banks of the Lee'. The *sean nós* singer Diarmuid Ó Súilleabháin often dropped in if he happened to be in the locality. The Daly and Creagh duet combination, noted for their lively rendering of Sliabh Luachra music, originated from these Cork-city sessions, and we formed the inevitable 'group': Ben Lennon (fiddle), Jackie Daly (accordion), Gary Cronin (fiddle) and myself (banjo), collectively known as The Shaskeen.

I've always been impressed with Ben Lennon's adherence to strict timing. A feeling for this essential element of the tradition can be gleaned from listening to fife band and pipe band drummers. Ben attributes this sense to his mother, Sally, who, he reckons, had metronomic timing. 'She was always drilling that into myself and Charlie.'

Ben and his brother Charlie, a noted fiddle player and composer, hail from Kiltyclogher in north Leitrim, a region renowned for its fiddle music. At one time Ben noted some fifty fiddle players in an area from 'Glenfarne to Kinlough, which would straddle most of north Leitrim'. A dancing

master, Seán O'Donahue, taught them the rudiments of music and Fermanagh fiddlers John Timmony, John Gordon and Francis John McGovern were frequent visitors. 'Francis John McGovern, a stonemason, was a great influence. He played pipes, fiddle and flute and had beautiful time, great time. Now, the one thing about the Fermanagh musicians, I always thought they had powerful time.'

The young Lennons had access to an old three-stringed fiddle which always hung on the kitchen wall. Ben remembers an evening when Francis John McGovern was asked to play one of Master Crowley's reels on this instrument: '"Well," he says, "I can't play her. She goes to the bass."' (Tunes were invariably referred to in the feminine gender around Leitrim and Fermanagh.) Only then did Ben realise that the fiddle required a fourth string.

He also remembers listening to stories about his grandfather endeavouring to learn tunes from visiting itinerant players. 'I used to hear my father talking about street musicians who came to the fairs. And there was two Donegal fiddle players; they were McCafferys. There was Red McCaffery and there was Black McCaffery. They would have been playing staccato style – Donegal style, you know. So we would have been playing a mix between the Sligo style, I suppose, and the northern style. And my grandfather used to follow them around the village when they'd be playing on fair days. That was the only way they could pick up the tunes. There was no tape recorder in those days. You just had to depend on your ear.'

Ben's father was a tailor by profession. Following in the paternal footsteps, he embarked on a career in the clothing industry, studying cutting and design in London for several years. From there he moved to Limerick and Cork and finally to a managerial post with Magee's of Donegal until his retirement in 1988. Constant movement enabled him to observe various musical styles and, while in Limerick, he regularly visited the Russell brothers in Doolin or Séamus Connolly in Killaloe and enjoyed playing for set dancing into the early hours with Paddy Canny and Francie Donnellan in east Clare.

Much of Ben's musical life is devoted to teaching traditional fiddle music and he holds master classes at the Willie Clancy and Drumshanbo summer schools. He acknowledges that his style, particularly the bowing techniques, is difficult to learn and many students, he finds, do not have the staying power to persist. 'The basic structure would be one of legato-style bowing with a weaving effect, rather than staccato which is just up and down bowing. That would have been the style which most of the legendary Sligo fiddle players (Coleman, Morrison and Killoran) would have adopted or used. Especially Coleman — a weaving. It reminds me of the clothing business. When you're weaving cloth or tweed you have the warp and the weft. The warp would be the long threads that run the length of the piece and the weft threads then go across. So it's up and over, maybe up one and under two, that type of thing. You get a different weave. That's what the bowing is like. It's an undulating kind of effect, you know.'

Although elements of Fermanagh and Donegal styles are evident, the intricate fiddle music from neighbouring Sligo made a lasting impression. Ben wishes he had been in their company when Michael Coleman and Jim Morrison were in their prime. 'A difficult music found nowhere else in the country at the time' is how he describes it. At a young age he sat listening to Michael Coleman playing 'Bonny Kate' and 'Jenny's Chickens' — the old 78 played on the gramophone for one full day. And his younger brother Charlie remembers being awakened at the age of seven in the early hours of the morning by an enthusiastic Ben having just heard Jim Morrison play 'The Dairy Maid'.

'I've listened to them inside out. Overall, Coleman would have to be the master, especially on his early records in the twenties. Some people, then, like James Morrison's music, more sharp and lifting, more suited now to flute playing. Paddy Killoran then had another way of playing, but the basic style was more or less the same. I think Coleman was able to camouflage what he was at. Every time you'd listen to it there was something else going on. It kept changing — wonderful variety in what he was doing. OK, there are five notes in a roll and that sounds very simple, but it's the way he played it and the way he attacked it. That's what I call a smothered roll. He had very fast fingering and on the treble he used a down bow instead of an up treble.'

A perplexing problem for many touches on the difference between traditional music and classical or art music. It's often said that all music is the same. Undoubtedly, styles of playing from different regions of the world spring from the same inspirational source, but jazz and classical musicians do encounter difficulties when attempting to play for traditional dancers. Ciaran Carson, in his book *Last Night's Fun*, cites the flawed attempts by musicians Yehudi Menuhin or James Galway to play 'simple' Irish hornpipes.

So what is this conspicuous peculiarity which characterises traditional music? In conversation between jigs and reels musicians often refer to the music as being clothed in *sean nós* (old style or way), or, as Ben Lennon would say, the music has 'the nya' in it. 'There are so many people who are beside something — what I call beside it — but they're just not in there. Just on the periphery but they never really got in. And it's like the set dancing today, for example. When I look and see them, it's a very mechanical thing they're doing. They're doing it all right but, when I think back on Kilkishen in east Clare and those people who used to dance the sets there, they had this kind of body language. You can't teach that. They were brought up with it and that's how they knew it. It was part and parcel of that whole "nya" thing and the music went with that.'

Mention of tradition brings to mind tunes good and bad. Ben possesses that rare ability to select fine tunes. His mentor, Francis John McGovern, also had this gift and 'would soon tell you if a tune wasn't much good'. Conversely, many inferior tunes may be righted if given proper treatment. 'It's the way they're treated,' Ben would say. In explanatory mode, he detects a similarity between the art of fine eating and the delicate handling of traditional melodies.

'The French are great now for food and wine. They spend two or three hours having a meal at evening time and they're just sipping away at the wine and they eat small little portions, not too much you know. They never get what you call full. Just nice, and it's all very subtle, what they're doing. And the savouring, the way they drink brandy and curl it around on the tongue. That's the way to play the music in my opinion. Savour the note and pick out the sweet notes in a tune and really emphasise them. And if you're in a session there with a tune for a while, just keep playing away — if you play it, you know, ten times — you just keep playing it and that's lovely. Sometimes I see now in sessions, they cannot get off the tune quickly enough to get on to another one. It's all about how many tunes they can play. And I hate that. I like to just play two or three tunes and play away at them and be in no hurry. And just savour this music . . . that's the way I see it.'

Like the term *ceol draíochta*, used in Clare and Galway, the word 'sweet' is often used around Sligo and Leitrim to describe quality traditional music. 'I don't think I've heard the expression *draíocht* here. But funnily enough, I think back to when I lived in Limerick and visited Doolin — I always remember the concertina player Packie Russell. I remember leaving the pub and the concertina music would be lingering in your head. It was a kind of lingering. There was something fairy-like about it. It stayed on when you had left . . .'

Tony MacMahon

BY FINTAN VALLELY

Possibly the best-known figure in Irish music, Tony MacMahon is its least visible icon. Most interviewed and quoted, he is often criticised and dismissed, yet remains its most articulate, respected and even feared ideologue. Uncompromisingly damning of superficiality, mediocrity, tokenism and Paddy-whackery, he simply defends the cultural patch which claimed him as a child.

Born in April 1939, Anthony MacMahon's journey in traditional music began as a metaphor for a life spent in recording and broadcasting. 'My earliest memory of traditional music is on a late summer afternoon when I was seven or eight. I remember standing at my hall door in the Turnpike in Ennis and hearing the most glorious sound I had heard in my lifetime. It was fiddle music from a gramophone coming from a house across the street. It wasn't just the music – it was more or less a call from a place that I felt was mine, a place in which I felt I could be home.'

His father P.J., of Irish-speaking parents from Kilmaley, was a small builder with a deep interest in traditional music. His mother, Kitty Murphy, played concertina, and, when travelling people visited, she would oblige them, 'playing standing up, with her leg on the second step of the stairs'. From Connolly, she was a first cousin to concertina-player Paddy Murphy and had been a neighbour of the noted fiddler Hughdie Doohan.

Tony's brother Chris was passionately interested in music too and organised accordion player Joe Cooley to visit: 'A young, blocky, low-set man wearing a grey two-piece suit and a white shirt with an undone collar and a rakish red tie and a head of fair hair and the most glorious smile.' For Tony, the music he played was 'an avalanche of experience that literally fell in on top of me'. In the years since, he has experienced the same *frisson* through the music of other players: 'There was total unity of every part of Cooley's body with the instrument as he played. Especially his face — his eyes, his mouth. His fingers always seemed to move in slow motion over the keys. He was a person to whom music was something altogether other than a series of notes, it was a spiritual experience that uplifted. It had a divine harmony.' Cooley visited the MacMahons regularly over his five years in Ennis. Working by day as a builder's labourer, and each night playing in a different house, passers-by would stop to listen through the door. 'Wherever he'd have the accordion left, that's where he would be the next night.'

Tommy Potts was brought to the MacMahon house too one winter afternoon, 'a tall, thin man with burning black eyes and wavy black hair and a slight stoop, carrying a fiddle case. He sat at the fire and played music that literally took me out of my seat.' Felix Doran was there once too, in 1952, in his white A40 van. Tony arrived home from school to find him playing in the kitchen. 'When he stopped playing, he put out his hands and I'll always remember him shaking my hand. It was like my hand was an insect in the middle of a great big shovel and when I opened my hand again there were four two-shilling pieces in it!'

Joe Cooley brought Tony his first accordion from London — a small piano-key. 'I had learned two tunes on the piano, so he put it on his knees longways, worked the bellows and I played my tune horizontally.' A button-box came from the piper Seán Reid, but perhaps anticipating her son's ultimate rejection of the instrument his mother hid it to preserve her ears from his obsessive self-teaching. His brothers Brendan and Christy played accordion too, and his sister Ita (mother of Tulla concertina player Mary McNamara) danced. Playing in the 1950s was not highly regarded — school friends and teachers at the Christian Brothers school jibed him for playing 'tinkers' music'. His father died when Tony was thirteen, this adding poverty to insecurity, and pressing music into emotional service. Playing was solitary, as well as social.

He went to Dublin in 1957 to train as a teacher at St Patrick's, Drumcondra. In the first week he located another legendary box-player, Sonny Brogan. Bill Harte he met and played with too: 'the only man that I ever knew who broke all the rules in that instrument and came up with something vibrant and new'. Tony was a regular caller to John Kelly's Horseshoe shop in Capel Street. 'John became a father figure to me. The advice he gave me when I first met him was to "learn to smoke a pipe and drink a pint"! He imbued me with a desire to search for a different kind of understanding in music — its historical and social context — because John was an enquirer.'

In 1963 Tony shared Séamus Ennis's apartment in

Bleecker Street in New York for a few weeks, learning from the master, being coached in the art of air-playing. 'He made me repeat the words over and over until I had them off by heart. "Now we'll start on the music," he said. He took me through "Bean Dubh a' Ghleanna" and kept me at it. He would say "put in the shiver there, boy, put in the shiver there".' Back in Ireland, he took up playing at O'Donoghue's in Merrion Row. He met Seán Ó Riada and singers from Coolea at the Oireachtas in the RDS and played for the composer's BBC sound recording of *The Playboy of the Western World.*

The summer of 1966 Tony spent in London. He played with Bobby Casey and recorded on the Topic record, *Paddy in the Smoke.* The fee from that purchased a tent and sleeping bags, and, with his brother Dermot and a friend, he spent three months driving to Tangiers. Walking around the Souk there, they were directed to a hashish cafe where they witnessed the blues of Morocco – the intense music of ud (lute) and dumbeq (drum). 'It was full of men sitting at tables. There were four musicians on a small platform at the front of the room and they were playing the most glorious music. In front of them there was a boy dancing the most sensuous, eloquent dancing I had ever seen. I had exactly the same experience as when I heard Joe Cooley the first time.'

Back in Dublin a year later, he got married to Kantha Naidoo, a South African. Piano player Bridie Lafferty hosted their wedding at Home Farm Road. John Kelly ran the show – it was a musical affair – and the wedding breakfast was lamb curry with rice and dhal, and a barrel of Guinness was the beverage. He ran a weekly session of traditional music and poetry at Slattery's of Capel Street in aid of the Defence and Aid fund for the African National Congress. The Tradition Club was to follow.

His first teaching job ended after his innovative artistic approach conflicted with clerical and departmental managers. Economic necessity saw him gigging professionally – not a popular thing at this stage – and, after one concert in Ennis, Comhaltas Ceoltóirí Éireann's magazine *Treoir* denounced him. Ever since 1969, he had been doing regular freelance presenting for RTE television, with seminal performers like Seán Ó Conaire and John Kelly on *Aisling Geal*, then *Ag Déanamh Ceoil* – where Clannad was the first group he introduced to camera. The exacting artistic standards set by producer Noel Ó Briain reinforced his own meticulousness in production, and his experience of having played with and known the definitive stylists in the music gave him a uniquely informed vision of which players were worth interviewing.

In 1974 he joined the RTE staff as radio producer and put *The Long Note* on the air. Later moving to television, his own most memorable achievement there is the television series *The Pure Drop*, wherein he had control of selecting performers and, over its seven years, feels that all the good players in the country were covered. 'We tended to steer away from the commercially successful and well recorded. When my successor in twenty years' time comes to make a programme such as *Come West along the Road*, it'll all be there, archived in the library.' *Come West* is a flashback series he is particularly proud of too.

His fear of performing on stage is overwhelmed by an artistic compulsion and desire to play, 'because I feel I have something to say musically that I cannot say any other way'. He dislikes the accordion, admiring the pipes and *sean nós* song. He does not shirk expressing personal political opinions, indeed this writer first witnessed him playing live in the Aula Maxima of UCD (now the National Concert Hall) in solidarity with striking students then occupying the building in 1969. Expressing his opinions from the stage, he feels, is part of his make-up as an artist necessarily engaging with the strife in his society. This, particularly around the time of the hunger strikes, he believes has blacked him from festival guest lists. 'The only stage I had at the time was in Germany with Micho Russell and Noel Hill.'

He believes that artistry is not essentially equated with, and may well be ill-served by, mere virtuosity. He cites Micho Russell as an exemplar of 'a wonderful unity of purpose; a most extraordinary spirit — even to listen to the cadence of his voice when he was talking to you about what he was having for breakfast. When he played he just took me to another world.' Despite the proliferation of more technically able musicians than ever before, he fears the music is 'in serious and terminal decline'. Few musicians excite him. Among those that do are piper Seán P.

McKiernan, fiddler John Carty, Frankie Gavin and the *sean nós* singers of Connemara: 'They bring out music that would swell your mind with oxygen.' For him, art should create a magic between the artist and the receptor. The absence of this is distasteful. 'I do believe that it has great magical powers to change the entire chemistry of the now. And that is the root of my abhorrence and anger with those who use music as cultural carpet or wallpaper.'

Quoted once as considering 'no boghole too deep for all the accordions in Ireland', the apparent paradox of this accordionist is explained by his perception of himself as trapped in that instrument as a vehicle for expressing his soul, and for touching hearts. Through the Cooley, Potts and Ennis soundscape of his childhood, the quivering diaphragm of the Turnpike gramophone transmitting Coleman's fiddle across the decades, the plucked and beaten metres of Islam — for Tony MacMahon, the instrument is but 'skeleton in which to carry the soul of music'.

Sing a song
for the mistress
of the bones

the player
on the black keys
the darker harmonies

light jig
of shoe buckles
on a coffin lid

FROM 'SAMHAIN' BY JOHN MONTAGUE

Néillidh Mulligan

BY FINTAN VALLELY

The name Mulligan is not found in the neon lights of traditional music PR, nor is it associated with the buzzwords of commercialism, but Dublin uilleann piper Néillidh Mulligan has been one of the best-known faces on the traditional music scene since the late 1960s. He was there at the founding *tionól* of Na Píobairí Uilleann and has rarely missed a gathering since. His brother Tom is also known internationally — for his music-venue pub, the Cobblestone, is in one of Dublin's oldest neighbourhoods, Smithfield Square.

Néillidh's story is best begun with the late Tom 'T.P.' Mulligan, for here was one of the great movers of the tremendously exciting and almost subversive social scene that the music occupied between the 1930s and 1970s. Séamus Ennis, Tommy Reck, Seosamh Ó hÉanaí, Tommy Potts, Breandán Breathnach — household names of the revival — were his compatriots. Music then was mostly played in private houses, laying the foundation for today's familiar session scene.

'Our grandfather could still play the concertina at 96; our mother Elizabeth McKeown and her sister Brigid from Barnacoola played melodeons,' says Néillidh's Uncle Colm. 'My father loved to play the flute but had fiddle too. There was always music in the house — I often fell asleep intoxicated with the bloody thing!' His father spent a lot of time away, working for long periods in America. Uncle John and Aunt Lizzie played fiddles too, she marrying into McNamara's Band, which had saxophone, trumpet and drums. Aunt Catherine played the concertina and took it to America, and, in the 1980s when she was nearly 100, she had it still in her room. Even though it was held together with sticking plaster she wouldn't give it up. 'I might play it again,' she would tell Colm. Another brother, Peter, lived to the age of 105 in Jersey.

There were uilleann pipers around them at the turn of this century, but Néillidh's father Tom – born in 1915 – didn't hear them until he witnessed Leo Rowsome at Mohill in 1932. Fiddle was the big instrument in his generation, and everyone learned. His brother Fran was the only one who sang, and his sister Lily learned fiddle later, in Dublin, from Frank O'Higgins, brother of Brian the versifier. Tom was taught by local fidle master Jack Conboy. They were resourceful too, for at the age of twelve Tom and Colm made fully functioning fiddles from tea-chest plywood: 'We bought strings, two and sixpence for a set, and the hairs of the bow were number ten thread rosined up good,' laughs Colm now. 'Tom was a genius at doing the scrolls – he needed no pattern to carve them.' In later years, indeed, Tom made pipe chanters.

Tom went straight from national school to work in Dublin in 1935, where he bought his first set of pipes from Abbeyshrule maker James Mulcrone, who was then living in Phibsboro. Chance threw him in with piper Tommy Reck with whom he formed a permanent friendship, playing with him, cycling to music pursuits, swimming, winning *feiseanna cheoil* duet awards. He was interested in the future and

survival of the music, in giving it expression and dignity, and so was involved in the Dublin Pipers' Club in the 1940s in Molesworth Street, and later in the Church Street Club.

Tom married Catherine MacMahon – then nursing in Holles Street – a cousin of writer Bryan MacMahon. Coming from a farm on the Cliffs of Dooneen at Beale, County Kerry, she extended Tom's music influences and opportunities. House-dances were also the scene of her upbringing too, and indeed from her own area she already knew Séamus Ennis because of his collecting travels. Emigration was common in her day, sometimes generating great excitement: her mother's sister in fact had eloped 'out the window to America,' she remembers. 'There was holy murder!'

The Mulligans set up home first in Cabra, down the street from pipe maker Matt Kiernan, moving then to Cabra Park. Néillidh's childhood had such a constant parade of musicians passing through that Séamus Ennis dubbed the home the 'Rotary Club'. Holidays in his younger days were spent in Kerry, later ones in Leitrim, but Connemara was his moulding place. Born with no Irish, Catherine and Tom reversed post-famine linguistic atrophy by taking family caravan retreats in Inverin for the summer months, Tom commuting there at weekends. Coláiste Lurgan was a focus then for other enthusiastic figures in music revival, dancer, singer and flute-player Paddy Bán Ó Broin among them – Paddy Bán's talented musical family were around in County Galway then. There were also the Lewises, *sean nós* singers Tom Pháidín Tom and Meataí Joe Shéamais, and piper Jim Dowling. Dublin sessions were numerous – in singer Larry Dillon's house in Monck Place, Phibsboro, in fiddler Jack Howard's and box player Mick Grogan's. All-Ireland *fleadhanna* brought them back south too, and in Beale once the Mulligans came upon fiddler John Kelly in the local pub in retreat from the madness of a Listowel *fleadh*. The bard was pontificating vigorously on the families residing on the distant Clare coast across the Shannon estuary.

Born in 1955, Néillidh was taught whistle by Ned Stapleton and Paddy Bán Ó Broin at the Church Street Club. He took up pipes at eleven, taught first by his father, then by Leo Rowsome at the school of music in Chatham Row. On Tommy Reck's advice, he was sent to the Dublin Pipers' Club Saturday classes, where he waited in line with Gay McKeon, Joe McKenna and Peter Browne. 'That way I learned two tunes every week!' he says. Leo's competition training saw Néillidh to Leinster *fleadh* victories, then an under-14 All-Ireland at Clones in 1968, and an under-18 at Listowel in 1970, which was his last: 'It was the same people going in there. You were competing with your friends. I just stopped,' he says. Competition for Néillidh had never been an egotistical pot-hunt: it marked challenge and achievement, and the carrying on and improvement of inherited music of which his father was proud.

Néillidh's first gig was at Tí Chúlain in Spiddal, but he went all over the country with his father, for by this time Tom had retreated back to fiddle in tandem with his son's ascent on the uilleann pipes. 'When I was with my father, you'd be constantly bumping into people who turned out then to be regarded as legends today! I remember meeting Ed Chisholm from New York who knew Michael Coleman. I met Lad O'Beirne once, up in Fred Finn's sister's house in Bunninadden.' Each year they met with Willie Clancy, after the Kerry *fleadhanna*, with the McCarthys over from London. Time was also spent with piper Felix Doran. 'The first time I heard him playing was with John Kelly in the Four Seasons in 1968.' And they knew *sean nós* singer Seán Ac Donncha of Ahascragh well. 'My father was a great man for jumping into the car – for Leitrim, Galway, wherever,' says Néillidh. 'Maybe down to play with Packie Duignan for a weekend, then he would come home as happy as Larry.' On his visits from the US Joe Heaney had them in his Gael Linn concerts with the Ní Dhómhnaills in Damer Hall, and it was the great singer's funeral in 1984 that was the occasion of Tom's last tune, for he died only two days later himself.

Perhaps the Mulligan connection with piper and folklorist Séamus Ennis illustrates their importance in music lore and, indeed, the smallness of the world. Séamus Ennis particularly relished playing the reel 'Miss Monaghan', on account of his mother being from that county. She had developed a friendship with Anne McKeown (Tom Mulligan's mother) through visiting her brother Frank McCabe, who was then on the run in

Bornacoola as a captain in the Volunteers. Frank taught the local pipe band and eventually married local Susie Conboy, sister of Jack who was later to teach Tom to play fiddle. Piper James Mulcrone, for whom Ennis tested pipes, eventually brought all this together, for he introduced Séamus to mother Ennis's old pal's son Tom at St Peter's Road, Phibsboro, in 1935. An intense and lasting friendship was formed. Often returning from collecting work in Connemara (he once cycled there), Séamus might arrive late at Tom's digs near Broadstone station, slip up the sash and into the bed beside him.

There was many a rendezvous too with the young Ennis and his father Jim in Cushion Doyle's pub. On one occasion, in the Ennis home at Jamestown, an inquest on Ennis senior's post-porter snack of 'porridge', which he shared with Tom and company, revealed that they had deprived the pups of a breakfast. There was swimming in Skerries, and there were trips in borrowed cars to Howth, jaunts all over the country, and high jinks and pranks that typically once saw Ennis in full bloom parading marches through the shocked 'quality' in a golf club. 'When Ennis got the car, we had great fun. He had Colm Ó Lochlainn's warpipes in the back, and this day in Rush he blew them up and drove them right through the crowd – in the front door and out the back! He did the same thing to us in Dromod one bank holiday – marched up and down playing outside the barracks at midnight,' Tom recalled in a 1983 interview.

Often, in later years, Ennis would stay for a fortnight in the Mulligan home, in between bouts of collecting.

Néillidh has many other connections in music. His uncle Alfie, whistle and flute player, has a pub in Leeson street – a renowned session house now where John Kelly junior plays regularly. And his namesake, Néillidh's brother Alfie, with brother Tom ran a famous music pub in Blackrock, County Louth, for a number of years; Alfie inherited Felix Doran's famous Rowsome-made pipes, that the piper had got in the 1950s at a cost of 150 guineas. Brother Tom runs the Cobblestone traditional music pub in Dublin's Smithfield. But it is Néillidh – heir to Séamus Ennis's Brogan set of uilleann pipes – who alone has made recordings. His first album, *Barr na Cúille*, came out in 1991 as a tribute to the home place and its legacy. His most recent, *Leitrim Thrush*, recalls the personalities of his growing up – Ennis, Reck, Rowsome and, in particular, his father Tom. He appeared once with Tom on UTV, and he was on Tony MacMahon's first programme *Glór* (Clannad's début too). He has played on *The Pure Drop*, *Cúrsaí* and *High Reel*, and also abroad on various Austrian stations.

Néillidh Mulligan misses solo performances of traditional music. 'Unless you're into buying and listening to CDs, there's no place to hear it. There's nowhere like Slattery's today. And music is all speeded up – everybody seems to have a bouzouki or guitar player in tow. I suppose that's why a lot of the singers and pipers formed their own organisations.' He is a consummate piper. For him it is a joyous process of constantly drawing on the lore he has accumulated since childhood, building on 'what I learned from the older players and singers, and what my father taught me. The respect they'd have for the music – that's an important thing.' Reedmaking and running repairs are part of the details of a piper's life – but essential to their musicianship. He teaches and gives workshops, at home and abroad, and is struck by the huge amount of interest in piping today. 'Séamus Ennis used to think the Northumbrian pipes were more suited to women! But there's a lot of young girls learning to play uilleann pipes now – a class I held in Celbridge had six girls, all under twenty. At the time of the first *tionól* in 1968, they reckoned there were about fifty pipers in Ireland. Now Na Píobairí Uilleann have possibly eight hundred pipers world-wide, four hundred of them in Ireland, and a big interest abroad.' Pipers' gatherings around the country are the art's life-blood. 'In the piping field you have to exchange lots of views. You have to watch people making reeds. You always learn something – everybody has some little bit to offer.' Performance and workshops can clash with the responsibilities of family life, and Néillidh only does what he has time for. But he still heeds T.P.'s advice: '"Never give up the day job!" Looking at Joe Burke and such people – I just couldn't do it.'

Néillidh Mulligan's performances in Estonia, Norway and New Zealand all add poignancy to the story of his father Tom's ebullient enthusiasm and gentle guidance. The music of Currycramp townland ('hill of the wild garlic') has been taken to Dublin and has added its own wild pungency there to the mosaic of migrants' music styles. Now in its fourth generation, through Néillidh and his brothers it is heard around the world.

Ann Mulqueen

BY FINTAN VALLELY

The intricate Cobh of Cork seems but shadows to gas
When compared with the proud, roaring falls of Dunass.

FROM 'THE FALLS OF DUNASS'

Wearing tights, short skirts, stiff petticoats and high heels, and being helped on to high, wobbly platforms in mucky tents by grinning old men: these are Ann Mulqueen's memories of the high life of the well-paid, dance/carnival 'spot' ballad singer in the transitional days between the *céilí* and the showband, when dancing was dancing and young people still knew ballads as 'singing'. Marquee tents were the bigger venues, and there were the faded parochial halls and purpose-built acreages of ball-room, recalling countless stories of rickety stages, players falling off the edge, and the tipsy *fear an tí*. In Tullylease in north Cork, the Ten-star Showband were half pop, half *céilí*, and every instrument had stars painted on it. The microphone was Heath-Robinson-ed from a bicycle dynamo, and, when the dance was over, the players slung their gear into coarse meal-bags and 'dragged them along after themselves and out the door'.

These were good gigs for a professional unaccompanied singer in the 1950s to 1960s, yet that time seems only a brief moment in Ann Mulqueen's life of song. Born at Castleconnell, County Limerick, in 1945, the first person she heard singing was her grandmother, and the first song she learned from her was 'The Falls of Dunass'. 'She was bred, born and reared beside the falls and had a great interest in local songs.' Ann's uncle from Limerick was particularly fond of hurling songs: 'As kids we used to really love Uncle Christy coming out at Christmas because he was a great singer and a great set dancer. We all have the five parts of the Ballyconnell set inside out from that.' But her father – a county council ganger – had no time for song. Pedantic about precision, he disliked lyrics that had been corrupted in handing on, but he read a lot, liked Dylan Thomas and Shakespeare and could deliver forty verses of Tennyson.

The touring Vic Loving Show's talent competition launched Ann. She had decided to enter when she was twelve. 'My sister Peggy said, "Sure, you can't sing at all!" And I said, "I can!" So she said, "Sing, so, till I hear you." And I sang "The Falls of Dunass" – I had just picked it up without learning it, my grandmother had sung it so often and talked about it so much. And Peggy looked at me – "Do you know, you *can* sing!" My mother was out in the kitchen the same day, up to her eyes in flour. Peggy went out and said, "Mam, do you know, Ann is a lovely singer?" "Arra, go away!" she says. Peggy says, "Will you just stop and listen for a minute?" So I went up on the table and I sang "The Falls of Dunass" and I saw my mother's face changing. The poor woman; there was nine of us – seven girls and two boys – and she was so busy all her life she never had any time to stop and think.' Off they went to the tent where the talent competition was being held: 'Half of us got in under the canvas because there was no money to go in. People there hadn't really heard of the song for an awful long time, and you could actually see the falls from where I was singing. I got a great reception!'

She got through to the semi-final and was the talk of the village: 'Slim Whitman was a big fella in those days, now, and they were all singing his songs.' This was 1956, and the rock-and-roll scene was obliterating older song and music, but it wasn't of any interest to Ann: 'I never went for it at all. I had some strange kind of a feeling about where I was living. And in actual fact I loved the river – the Shannon flowed by my house.' From there she became obsessed with learning local songs, and then in 1959 Donal Ryan from Parteen in County Clare across the river took her to the *fleadh* in Thurles. Mistakenly entered in the senior competition, she sang 'The Falls of Dunass' and 'The Hills of Sweet Mayo', which her brother had brought back from Mayo-men working in England. 'The others were all singing things like "Danny Boy" – there wasn't one traditional song sung at that All-Ireland.' Séamus Ennis and Seán Ó Síochain were adjudicating, and Ennis gave the verdict. 'Well, guess who won?' She repeated this performance the following two years at Boyle and Swinford.

'If I was asked what was the biggest change I've seen over the years, it would be that it was impossible to get a song in those days. I often waited two years. I would hear the person singing it at a session, and I might have been a bit shy that time to approach an adult, so I'd wait till the next *fleadh* – hoping that I might see the man again.' She spent months trying to get 'The Streams of Bunclody'; eventually it came from Dubliner Jim Crystal to whom she wrote after hearing him on the radio. Tortured indeed by that song's beauty, she recalls her craving for it: 'My mother said to me, "Can you think of any line of it?" and I'd sing the line that would affect me most and she'd say, "Ah, Jesus, we'll have to get it!"'

Her mother had become completely involved and was Ann's sole support at a time when no one of her generation was singing traditional song. From near Castleconnell herself, she was a set dancer. Her brother Mikey played accordion and so she knew all the tunes and used to lilt for her daughters dancing in the house. Like all her sisters, Ann had been doing step dancing with Miss Fitzgerald since she was nine – indeed some sixty girls danced locally. Highlight of the week was Seán Ó Murchú's *Céilí House* on Saturday nights. 'Our friends would come in and we'd have all our shoes lined up, light and heavy, and we'd dance all through that programme.'

Céilíthe were the popular social dance then, with a singer who sang in waltz time as part of the band. Good singers were scarce, and Ann was a popular 'spot' artiste at many of these and at showband dances too. 'If you sang at a *céilí*, that was the end of you. One adjudicator used to always say my style was "changing" and it was "because of the *céilí* bands" that I was "swinging the traditional songs". But I had my selection of traditional songs aside that I never used for

dances!' In fact, so little did she 'swing' any songs at the dances that 'I'd have to bring one sister along especially to stop the piano player. They used to think I was out of time and would be trying to bring me into time with the piano.'

Able to please nobody, she had to keep her 'odd' singing a secret from her friends. 'I would have been about fifteen then, and I'd be embarrassed sometimes because my friends would be laughing at the type of singing I was doing.' She sang spots with the Dixielanders, among others, often getting five pounds per night, which she used to pay the seven and sixpence for her own and her two sisters' secondary education. One night at Caherconlish, a spot with the Gallowglass Céilí Band landed her an offer to tour with them. 'I was only about fifteen, but he offered me fifty-seven pounds a week and my digs free, and I'd have to live in Naas. Jesus, I thought I'd never get home at all! At two o'clock I woke up my mother and told her the money I was offered. She said to my father, "Wake up, John Joe, you're a poor man no more!" The Reverend Mother came up to my mother and she said, "Mrs Mulqueen, are you out of your mind to let a young little girl all over the country – with a crowd of thugs?" Now The Gallowglass were the furthest you'll get from a crowd of thugs, but they were like U2 today.'

This was a big event for the village, for bands appeared mysterious and romantic in their uniforms and decorated transport. Crowds turned out to see Ann off to Naas. With the Gallowglass she travelled all over the country, singing a song for every county in waltz time – 'Beautiful Bundoran' in Donegal, 'The Hills above Drumquin' in Tyrone. Pat McGarr billed her on posters as the 'fifteen-year-old wonder', other promoters called her the 'girl with the golden tonsils', and, of course, 'queen of song'. She stayed for three months' trial, but found the life intensely lonely. 'Six nights a week and in bed every day till about four. It was very bad weather, some nights you wouldn't have enough sleep – *céilís* at that time were sometimes from eight until two. We always came back to base in Naas.'

She quit, but couldn't adjust to normal life, so she left school and took up hairdressing. She still sang at *céilíthe* and never missed a *fleadh*. Once she arranged a lift back from Enniscorthy with a respectable Comhaltas Ceoltóirí Éireann official who was sharing a room with a Dublin piper, but after the final *céilí* the driver still hadn't turned up. 'We decided we would go up to the boys' room and see if they were gone. So here was this set of pipes inside and I said, "They're not gone." We were jaded after going around all day, so in the two of us went to the bed. We had a great sleep, and at about four in the morning the two boys arrived back. The piper decided he'd play us a slow air on the pipes – "Blind Mary". The next thing the manager came up. He busted in the door and he gave a look at the two of us inside in the bed, "And two women with ye! Get out! We want none of your type here!" We had to get up, dress ourselves, and he marched the four of us down the stairs in front of all the musicians!'

All the time she was learning new songs. She'd learn the air first, then go over all the turns to get it right, maybe having to amend it once she'd got the words. She learned 'Dark is the Colour' from Willie Clancy, got others at ballad nights in the Silver Springs and The Lakeside, where she sang with Clancy and Joe Heaney. She substituted for Dolly MacMahon with the Dubliners and lost her job three times. She sang in the Bunratty cabaret by night and – for her employer – dressed their ringleted hairpieces by day. In 1965, she went to England with the Brosna Céilí Band where Mick Burke (fiddler Kevin Burke's father) got her into the Hibernian Hall in Fulham Broadway. She sang there at weekends for two years with Roger Sherlock, Kevin Taylor, John Bowe, Oliver and Raymond Roland, Seán Maguire and Josephine Keegan.

Back in Ireland in 1967, she sang in the cabaret at Cruise's of Limerick. She married in 1969 and moved to Ring, County Waterford, where her Kerry husband Tomás was teaching and had a pub, An Tigín Cheoil. She learned to speak Irish from scratch and now a lot of her song repertoire is in Irish, and she is currently on the board of Teleifís na Gaeilge. During their seven years running the bar, the Tóibín family were regulars. They were all singers and sang anything they liked, 'Nioclás doing "Lili Marlene" and "Mockingbird Hill" with the grace notes and stops, the same as if he'd been singing "Sliabh na mBan!"' Ann benefited from their huge repertoire in both languages, and there there were many other singers – Willie Hally, Pádraig de White, Cath Tobin, the Conneelys.

Singing at dances in her teenage years was good fun, as the nation fashioned its new-found public-entertainment practices. Arriving late added spice, faraway places had a huge loading of romance. The pleasure was intensified by the hardship – cars without heaters on two-hundred-mile journeys; envying the locals the nearness of their cosy beds; home late and only just warmed up and having to go off to the day-job. She sang regularly on Comhaltas tours – England, Europe, America, Ireland – up until ten years ago. These days she hosts a local traditional music radio show and guests at traditional singing weekends all over the country. She adjudicates too, acutely conscious of the

potential for damage to young the people's egos. She finds songs a great comfort, and particularly since the death of a sister, when many of them have taken on new, unexpected meaning and intensity. 'With television there's no doubt about what you're watching, but with song words you can imagine anything.'

Treasa Ní Cheannabháin
and
Róisín El-Saftay

BY FINTAN VALLELY

Forty-five miles west of Galway city the town of Cill Chiaráin is locked into the Connemara Gaeltacht by a tangled spaghetti of narrow roads to the north, and decorated by the reclining grace of the Aran Islands to the south. This isolating geography has protected the language of Ireland from easterly onslaught, and its rocky topography has placed it beneath the line of vision of conquistadores – in fact, just one step from hell, according to the seventeenth-century Cromwellians.

Now the centre for the Irish language broadcasting media, Connemara has rustled and broken micro-technology to promote everything that should logically have been suffocated by electronic mass-communication. Key to its cultural life is song in Irish, and the pillar of that is what is known as *sean nós* (literally 'old style'). This has a high nasal timbre that tongue and epiglottis carefully turn around inside the singer's mouth cavity like savoured brandy. Rich ornament, extended vowels, absence of hurry and almost mesmerised self-absorption lend this song style archaic resonance with Islamic chant and west African folksong. The survivor of a golden age of an art of singing perhaps once familiar all over the island prior to the seventeenth century, here it is preserved by terrain, and survives by having meaning.

Into its ambience Treasa Ní Cheannabháin was, 'as Joe Heaney would say, bred, born and buttered' in 1951. At the age of nine, a scalding incident kept her off school for several weeks. Confined to the house she had time to reflect and was notably impressed by her mother. 'My father was probably in England that year, but she'd start her cleaning and she'd be singing – "Stephen Foster", "Stranger on the Shore" – popular songs from her day. She had *sean nós* songs as well, but she didn't sing an awful lot of them.' Later she did try to teach Treasa *sean nós* – 'Sail Óg Rua' was her first song.

Duffy's circus launched her into taking singing seriously. 'The ringmaster invited any singers to come up in a competition, so I decided I'd like to go. I sang a Jim Reeves song and I won!' The power of national radio at that time exposed everybody to popular music. Growing up in a culture where song was dominant was just a perfectly natural thing to be doing, regardless of lyrics and style. Perhaps there were deeper resonances, though. For *sean nós* is lyrical and personal – just like much modern popular song – utterly different to the useful practicality of the English-language, literal ballad which is the mainstay of traditional song elsewhere.

House gatherings saw musicians calling in to Treasa's home, and *sean nós* song would be sung. Her mother and Joe Heaney were second cousins, related to Josie Seán Jack. Treasa's father sang too, but not *sean nós*, and her first cousin is singer Peadar Ó Ceannabháin. The national media influenced *sean nós* too. 'We were exposed to *sean nós* from Ciarán Mac Mathúna's *Ceolta Tíre* and *Céilí House*. When Joe Heaney or Johnny Joe Phatchín or Darach Ó Catháin or the likes of those people would be singing, there'd be total silence in the house. We would have respect for this singer, and we'd be told who this singer was, what the song was about. I have very vivid memories of going to sleep on a Saturday night listening to those programmes.'

Joe Heaney she respects for having had the courage to face down lack of interest in his art at home, and go to America and teach *sean nós*: 'The people over there missed what they had left behind and they appreciated it in him. Joe Heaney made his fame because he went somewhere else.' She is quite clear that present-day *sean nós* singers have only been able to 'come out' since the setting up of Radio na Gaeltachta in 1972. When she was growing up, there were few *céilí* dances to go to, as the culture was mainstream. 'We'd dance to Joe Dolan or Johnny McEvoy.' Records of traditional music or singers were scarce. A few people had music on reel-to-reel tape, others had a handful of Gael Linn recordings of Heaney.

As children, Treasa and her sisters learned step dancing, but older people did *sean nós* dance: 'One man in particular, Tomás Cheata Breathnach – he had this big moustache like James Connolly – from Árd Mhór, a very old man when I was a young girl. He would dance at the racing regatta in Cill Chiaráin. Pádraig Tom Phatch would be playing the accordion, and Tomás Cheata would do the *sean nós* dance and do it spectacularly. He used to do it every year that we had the regatta – so beautifully – so that even though you only saw this display once a year the steps stayed with you.'

Like the song, the *sean nós* dance was by then considered

archaic, even if interesting. Such was the case up to the 1970s, 'because the traditional music first of all started to make a comeback, then you'd have traditional singers that would sing in a pub and get the silence.' Micheál Ó hÉidhín, now a Department of Education school music inspector, was the first person living locally to teach instrumental music in Carna.

In 1970, Donncha Ó Súilleabháin, secretary of An tOireachtas, suggested Treasa enter the competition. 'I thought the Oireachtas was for old people – old men. I went that year and I was impressed by it and I enjoyed what I saw. There was only one judge, and they'd just say, "Is there anybody else that wants to come up and sing?"' This easygoing attitude persisted until RnaG's recording the event demanded that order be put on it. Treasa didn't win anything, but it intensified her interest. After leaving college in 1973, she taught for a couple of years in Kylemore Abbey, then she taught in an Irish-speaking school in the Rosport, Belmullet, area of the Mayo Gaeltacht, driving more than a hundred miles a day. This was a considerable strain, and the fact that not all students had Irish meant that the added demands of bilingualism seriously damaged her throat and silenced her song for some time.

In 1995 she won Corn na mBan at the Oireachtas, and came second in the prestigious Corn Uí Riada to Dubliner Mairéad Ní Oistín. She has no particular love for competition, but feels that *sean nós* needs an inspirational platform. '*Sean nós* would be dead and buried years and years

ago only for the Oireachtas. It has a lot of faults and we have all been giving out about it, and the rules have been silly at times. I haven't agreed with the adjudication at times. People like to go and listen to the competition – and it's not the same as going to a concert.' She acknowledges that adjudication brings out conflicts with those who believe that *sean nós* is something one is born with, and it does no justice when a good singer is simply off form on the day. She realises too that there is no one central style. 'You'd really need an adjudicator that knows the Donegal *sean nós* and knows the Donegal songs. How would I know if their accent is not absolutely right?' For herself, when teaching *sean nós*, 'I go to it with the accent that I have and I try to teach it with the accent that I have.'

Disputes rage too about the validity of modern *sean nós* lyrics, and how the singer should perform. One of Treasa's favourite singers while in college was Caitlín Maude. 'I used to love watching her sing, because she would put so much feeling into it. She had long hair and she'd be singing – say "Bean Uí Raghallaigh" – and her whole body was in it.' It is this aspect of performing *sean nós* that disturbs her where judging is concerned. 'They say you shouldn't be moving your face, that you should stand up there and sing the song without putting too much emotion into it. But these songs are very emotional! It shouldn't matter how you're dressed or how your facial expression is – it's the song that they are supposed to be adjudicating.' Authenticity, getting the correct version, learning a wrong version from a parent, mixing up songs – all are issues of debate. Each song has its integrity, its logical story, that makes no sense if corrupted.

For Treasa's daughter Róisín, those exhausting drives through Mayo are remembered differently. 'She'd be singing away and I'd be in the back. She'd call me up to the front and I'd have my arms around her neck, and I'd be learning whatever it was. And I'd be trying to be so like my Mum was, singing – so sweet and up so high. And that's how I learned my first *sean nós* song – standing – Mum driving the car and me hanging onto her neck repeating what she was singing line by line – "An Sagairtín", that was my first "proper" song.'

Now Róisín teaches song to 6- to 15-year-olds herself. She might begin with 'Cúnla', or perhaps 'Sí do Mhamó í', and they copy it on tape and learn by ear. 'I explain the whole thing to them and the beats – it's important for them to have the beats. Certain words will kind of be skipped with one note – there might be three words with one note. I take each line as I sing it and point out what I do to it as I sing it. Each line is different.'

Her *sean nós* repertoire would run to perhaps fifteen Connemara songs. She will chip away at new ones, but it is a slow process. She still learns from her mother. 'I need my master to sit down beside me and do the words, so I know what they're saying.'

Competition for Róisín was a challenge. 'It meant that I had to practise more; and had to learn more songs as quickly as I could so that I wouldn't be going up singing the same song the whole time – and people getting sick of it. Also it was an opportunity to meet other young people learning the songs and singing *sean nós* too. When I started off, I was the only one in Castlebar of my age in my school that knew what *sean nós* was – let alone how to sing it.' In Connemara there are many young people learning and singing, 'but they have not yet come out in public; not only in competition, but they might even be afraid singing in the pub. So you wouldn't be sure who has got it and who hasn't.' She herself won the under-15 and under-18 All-Ireland *sean nós*, but has had difficulties with English-language song. 'I never got anywhere much with the English. People used to say to me I was putting too much ornamentation into it. It put me off learning English songs so much!' Nobody at her college in Galway that she knows of sings *sean nós*. She often even has to explain to friends what it is.

Treasa too has had a good response from children she has taught. 'Even those with no *sean nós* in their blood at all, they were really picking it up.' She has found great enthusiasm among children and their parents. Both Treasa and Róisín have definite ideas as to what can be done with *sean nós* and what shouldn't. For Róisín, it has to be solo, 'no music, no accompaniment! There has to be a certain amount of twirls in it – that's the only way I can explain it. I try to sing it as close to the style of Connemara and that's what I hear. I wouldn't sing it any other way.' Even so, she acknowledges that each time new people come to *sean nós* 'they put their own style on it'.

In 1998 Róisín can confirm that, when teaching the lower age groups, there are fewer boys — possibly to do with the breaking of the voice. However, in the context of competitions, she asserts: 'When I go to the Oireachtas now I think women have taken over the shop.' Quite a turnaround from when Treasa first went there and mostly men were involved. 'I think the men used to be winning all the time too and it kind of put the women in the shade. Then all of a sudden the women started winning and the men are starting to disappear now!' Both Treasa and Róisín sing *sean nós* song socially and teach it all over the west and at summer schools. They acknowledge that there is something distinctive in *sean nós* song that must be preserved if the term is to mean anything at all. Change may be inevitable, but it should be slow. Treasa's children's name is El-Saftay, as they are Egyptian by birth but her three youngest children will enter their teenage years with the music of Connemara most familiar to their ears, and Róisín has already begun her adult life as an accomplished *sean nós* singer.

Maighread Ní Dhómhnaill

BY FINTAN VALLELY

Maighread Ní Dhómhnaill has been part and parcel of the folklore of Irish music for more than twenty years. As a schoolgirl, with sister Tríona and brother Mícheál, she sang with the memorable Skara Brae in 1972. She had a solo album in 1976, another in 1991, and she featured on the best-selling compilation *A Woman's Heart* in 1995. Equally at home in Irish or English, with traditional or contemporary song, Maighread and Tríona together produce a synergistic energy which expands their heart-gripping voices in duet performance, yet each retains a distinctive personal delivery and timbre. Maighread and her brother share a great story of interactions of culture and relocation, history and geography, parental dedication and liberal upbringing.

'My father was born in Rannafast, County Donegal,' says Maighread. 'His parents, with my aunt Neilí, got a land grant in Baile Gib, County Meath; they were part of Dev's relocation of Gaeltacht people to try and bring the Irish language to the east coast. But they missed the mountains and sea so much they only lasted ten or fifteen years and moved back.' But by the time they decided to sell up and move back, their son Aodh – Hiúdí Mhicí Hiúdí, Maighread's father – was married to a Dublin woman, Bríd Comber, and was teaching in nearby Kells.

Herself a passionate Gaelgóir, Bríd had worked in the Department of Education in the capital city. There, with Seán Ó Casaide (father of Na Casaidí), Seán Ó Síocháin and Séamus Ó Tuama, she had sung with Cór Chraobh Uí

Chétinnigh of Conradh na Gaeilge and broadcast on Radio Éireann as Na Fánaithí. 'We might have been the pioneers of an "Irish" group,' she says. 'There weren't too many at it then in the mid-fifties!' Born in Gurteen, County Sligo, her own mother had family connections with Michael Coleman and played melodeon. Bríd's childhood is vivid with house-céilíthe during the holidays, lancers and half-sets. 'And to think that my own children's generation think that they founded all that!' she quips. Brought up in Dublin, the war years gave her many visits to Coláiste Ghaeilge Bhaile Ghib, 'on bicycles, there was no transport', and it was there that she met Aodh, her husband-to-be.

Aodh was obsessed with the language and customs of his childhood, and from June until September each year he relocated the Ó Dómhnaill children in Rann na Féirste, while he taught in the Coláiste Gaeilge there. A singer himself who played flute and accordion, he was assistant head at the Kells vocational school and a devoted collector of folklore and song. In his twenties he began collecting for the Folklore Commission, carrying a heavy 'Ediphone' wax-cylinder recorder on the back of his bicycle – graduating in later years to a tape machine.

'He was the first person to collect from Tory Island [off Donegal] – he brought out *The Cáilín Gaelach*. He transcribed the stories of Sorcha Chonaill and the songs of Máire John, his aunt. And he was writing articles too, for *Béaloideas*. All his diaries are in the Folklore Department in UCD,' says Maighread. This constant subconscious immersion in Gaelic language and singing had a profound influence on the girls. 'We were reared literally from the cradle, from the time we could walk, to the notion of *sean nós* singing. We were trotted around all the different houses in Donegal. Without knowing "how", we just knew the songs. We don't remember learning.'

Back in Kells for the rest of the year, with the hard slog of rearing and education, their mother Bríd was an equally strong educative influence: 'Mother had not a "traditional" voice. She had come to Irish song through Seán Óg Ó Tuama, the *feis* and singers like Máire Ní Scolaí. But from a singing point of view, her influence was incredible.' Bríd's experience was in light classical music, so she was able to introduce another level of performance expertise and expressive repertoire to her children, complementing their holiday immersion in *sean nós*.

There were other influences too. 'There in Kells, Daddy would get together next-door neighbours, other teachers, people who had an interest in Irish songs, in a *clais cheadáil* – a unison choir, no harmonies,' says Tríona. 'They would be practising every week all throught the winter months for the Oireachtas.' These brought travel too, and a series of mid-fifties awards. Another influence too was their grandmother. 'People would come into the house just to see her, and she would sing "Follow Me up to Carlow", "Lambs on the Green Hills", "Toora Loora Loora Loo", and she'd do all the actions for them!' says Maighread. 'And when the lads would be going off to work in Scotland they'd have asked her, "What do you want?" She'd say, "I want a song." And they brought her back songs.' Later on, they were to discover – to their surprise – that their Aunt Neilí also had a vast store of songs, particularly songs in English.

Maighread and Tríona 'went to the nuns' too for music and 'classical' piano lessons when at school, and Tríona alone still sticks with 'the dashboard', but their education in song was mostly oral.

While still at school, Maighread, Tríona and brother Mícheál responded to the times and joined with Gaeltacht friend Dáithí Sproule, singing harmonies à la Beatles and using guitars, as the group Skara Brae. 'We had begun to hear the songs, get versions from Daddy,' says Maighread. 'We put them together with guitars and a few harmonies. I was fifteen when we did the album.' Now re-released on CD by Gael Linn, Maighread sees it as a kind of land-mark. 'I think Skara Brae is wonderful as an archive piece. But I listen to it now and I can't believe that it's actually me. It's so hesitant, nervous. I sound very unsure of myself – which I was!' She is much more critical of her first Gael Linn album: 'I was starting off; I was a very immature singer. But Skara Bare was fun – I have great memories of what we did. And I realise too that we were among the first to put guitars to the old songs. It was a time that was so important for all of us.'

Skara Brae was wound up when she went to study nursing. Then she married Belfast-man Cathal Goan, presently director of Teleifís na Gaeilge, and had two children. Still she pursued singing, without regrets, through The Tradition Club in Slattery's of Dublin. 'In seventy-three to five I met Joe [Holmes], Eddie Butcher, Geordie Hanna – listening to them, getting recognition. From singing together I had to learning to sing on my own.' And by 1980 she could support The Chieftains in the Sense of Ireland concert in London's Albert Hall.

Her first Gael Linn recording she feels was outside her control, but for the second she chose and organised the material and accompaniment herself. 'I wanted it to be about love, women and women's songs', she says. 'I felt it was like a mission, I wanted to do it right.' She wanted Tríona to be involved too, and Mícheál and Donal Lunny. She had to keep the home running and hold on to the day job. 'After Tríona went to America I had always felt my other half was gone. This would be the first time we'd sung together for fourteen years; it was like a homecoming,' she relates. Over the two weeks' recording, Maighread worked in the hospital theatre from 8 am until 1 pm, then she was in the studio at 2.30 for the next twelve hours. Her determination paid off in the quality of that album, most of its songs a tribute to her sightless Aunt Neilí's meticulous memory for nuance, pitch and detail and her vast archive of Irish, and phonetically remembered English, song ('Knickers of Corduroy' is the last song she gave to Maighread).

Maighread and Tríona both feature also on one of the Wyndham Hill *Celtic Christmas* recordings produced by

Mícheál. On the first of these, Maighread premiered the Kilmore (Wexford) carol, *Third Carol for Christmas Day*, in a setting by Donal Lunny. The sisters are gigging together now whenever possible – mostly unaccompanied songs, their repertoire from teenage years. But because Tríona has been out of Ireland and Maighread herself has not been performing much, 'we can get away with doing our old songs – they're new to a lot of people. Young kids don't remember the Bothy Band, they don't remember Skara Brae. To them it's all fresh and different!'

In May of 1997 the giant Japanese JVC corporation licensed Maighread's Gael Linn album and brought her out to showcase it with Donal Lunny in Tokyo and Osaka. In August she sang again at an Earth Celebration Festival with the Koto drummers of Sado island. She has been singing a lot more in recent times, all over the country, guesting a lot with Lunny's band – at the Tonder festival, and two tours in the US in 1998. She feels it is 'a unique opportunity to be able to sing with such an accomplished band. It takes the whole thing onto a different level.' Unaccompanied song restricts her to 'small venues, small audiences – it is very individual, and there's only a certain number of places you can do. But when I sing with the band I perform in venues with large audiences.' Mindful of source, she still mixes styles, enjoying Lunny's exotic arrangements, but 'I always make a point of doing one song on my own, unaccompanied, or with maybe just a synth (synthesiser) drone.' She is delighted that her Gael Linn album is also licensed 'out of existence' in the US at the moment. 'There are tracks from it available from five different record companies. The last time I was over I was amazed to see something from it in nearly every shop I went into – Celtic this, Celtic that.'

At the moment she is planning a new album. 'I have moved into something different from *Gan Dhá Phingin Spré*, the last recording. I'm afraid that because it has been so well received and successful I'll never be able to produce anything like it again. But I would love to continue in that mode and bring it a step forward. In the past when I would get up to sing, I thought that you just got your voice and you sang your song. Now I realise that that's just not enough. You have to know how to perform it – to project, use a microphone. Touring and being on the road and doing big concerts gives you that. Now that I have so much more experience, going into the studio this time will be different.'

Possibly the most difficult thing Maighread Ní Dhómhnaill has done in her life is uprooting and moving to Galway. 'When you've lived in a city for twenty-five years, you find that the country is extraordinarily isolated.' She also gave up the nursing career – which she had once given up the music for – but doesn't miss that at all. 'I had toyed with the idea of giving it up for several years, because I was always afraid that I might lose both. But when I quit I found that I just moved into the music. I have freedom to do so much more. I am now available – whereas before I was always jockeying things around.'

Maighread always sings around the house, and listens to song constantly. 'I couldn't survive without it — it's my way of expressing myself.' A good song for her is 'something that grabs you — that moves you. When I listen to Joe Heaney, something stirs inside me. Something like that doesn't happen too often. Len Graham always does it to me, Elizabeth Cronin had it, and Róise na nAmhrán. And my Aunt Neilí had style — the way that she sang grabs you. I've always adored listening to Joni Mitchell for that. Mary Smith from the Isle of Lewis in Scotland has something very special for me too.'

Mairéad Ní Mhaonaigh

BY FINTAN VALLELY

At the turn of the century An Píobaire Mór, the Donegal piper Turloch Mac Suibhne, lived at Luinneach, Gweedore. With the dignity of the dispossessed chieftain that he was, he took his profession very seriously and wore a tall hat and tails. One night in his sportier days he found himself playing in the home of a Protestant clergyman, and so impressed with him was the daughter of the house that she decided he was the man for her and came after him. As a token of good faith he demanded that she throw away her shoes, so she did. Unable to marry in her father's church, she 'turned' Catholic and stayed with the Mooney family until the wedding.

Three generations later, Mairéad Ní Mhaonaigh, whose great-grandmother, Róise Mhór Ní Bhraonáin, it was who took in Mac Suibhne's wife-to-be, is known among followers of traditional and folk music all over Europe and the US as fiddler and lead vocalist with the group Altan. An old neighbour in Mairéad's childhood told of how An Píobaire had brought the 'boortree' (elder) to the area in order to have a supply of cane for making his pipe reeds. Her father Francie's mother had played concertina, and he was a fiddler. Born in 1959, she had known songs of the area from a young age, but only began to learn to play at eight or nine after visits to fiddler Joe Jack Curran's in Magheragallon. Francie visited there once a week to clear his head of school-teaching with reels and 'highlands' (strathspeys).

The children were taught the local dances by their

mothers. 'In the beginning I thought music was just for old people, but Joe Jack's family were all singers and played whistles, so that made me interested, because it was someone of my own age playing and singing: myself and my brother Gearóid, and our first cousins the Dinnys [Gallachóirs] used to come down as well – Margaret, who plays the bodhrán, and her father, Jimmy Dinny. Jimmy was Joe Jack's brother-in-law, and he had amazing songs.'

Jimmy Dinny was himself amazing, for he had got all his songs from his father who had died when Jimmy was just nine. 'He had a couple of hundred versions of songs in English and Irish. They didn't have tape recorders, so it was a matter of memory – you just assimilated it. He told us that his father had sung all the time – and Jimmy himself did the same thing. I remember I used to be sitting in the house and he'd sing "Tiocfaidh an Samhradh" just as we were making tea – and he was after working with the hay, so it was real. He was after singing something about what he was doing and it all made so much connection.' Jimmy's song triggers could generate other reactions too, for once, waiting for a train in Edinburgh station with Mairéad's aunt during the war, he was inspired to sing 'Sweet Caroline of Edinburgh Town': 'This woman came up to him crying and she said, "I'm Caroline's daughter." That meant so much to Jimmy. And he had all those stories that connected his songs with the reality.'

For Jimmy, singing wasn't simply for performance, it was something done at will. 'It was very important at that age to know that he was making the things in songs real rather than just something from past generations. Sometimes my father would do the same thing. We'd be down in Magheragallon or some place and my father would say, "That's the Binn Bhuí where the Dúlamán used to be collected." So that was the song "Dúlamán na Buinne Buí" for me. He could be telling me yarns, but to me he was making it real. And "Báidín Fhéidhlimidh" – "There's Gola there. Báidín Fhéidhlimidh went over to Gola."'

By the age of ten, Mairéad was playing fiddle too, taught by her father. But the critical boost to her enthusiasm didn't happen until 1973, on her first trip to Dublin with her father and mother for a Comhaltas concert at which she was singing. There she heard Paddy Glackin and Tony Smith playing fiddles. 'It was just the most amazing thing. I had never heard anything like it – and they were young! So as soon as I went home then I started playing again and I couldn't stop. My friends thought I was loop-the-loop, because all they wanted to do was go out to dances, and all I wanted to do was go to sessions.'

Mairéad's father taught in a school at Luinneach, up near the Bloody Foreland. In younger years he had been involved in drama and play-writing for Aisteoirí Ghaoth Dobhair. Out of this came the song 'Gleanntáin Ghlas Ghaoth Dobhair'. 'He wrote that on his honeymoon! The Aisteoirí were going to Glasgow to play for the Gorbals emigrants, so somebody said to Daddy, "You should write a song for the ones over in Scotland." He took "Paddy's

Green Shamrock Shore" as the air and just put his words to it. Performed first in the Gorbals!'

Fiddler Dinny McLoughlin from Buncrana was her next inspiration. He passed on 'other techniques that my father wouldn't have – like rolls and bowing. And tunes that I didn't know.' From then on the Mooneys exchanged alternate weekends with the Buncrana people, and around the same time Dermy Diamond and Tara Bingham (fiddle and flute, from Belfast and Comber) began visiting, with Belfast banjo player Gerry McCartney and fiddler Andy Dickson. Through them Mairéad was introduced to tunes from down south that they'd picked up at *fleadhanna*. Veronica and Bernadette Smith from Armagh brought yet other tunes learned through the Armagh Pipers. Other music came from the radio, particularly from Radio Na Gaeltachta.

When secondary education led to college, Mairéad's priority was 'Where was the best music being played?' In Dublin, when she was at teacher training college from 1979 to 1980, she knew fiddler Nollaig Casey, who had begun playing with the orchestra and who busked and played sessions with her. Frankie Kennedy was then a regular visitor to Dublin at weekends, and they played together, sometimes appearing on posters. 'I was "called in" in college one time, and was told "I don't like one of my students playing music full time." And when I said, "I'm not playing full time," she told me "I hear you're busking in the Dandelion Market." I was just devastated!'

Married to Frankie Kennedy in 1981, she got a job straight from college, working with him at St Oliver Plunkett's National School in Malahide. Moving Hearts piper Declan Masterson taught there too, and fiddler Máire O'Keeffe started at the same time. Teaching for ten years – an understanding headmaster made life easy – and a career break in 1987 gave both Mairéad and Frankie the courage to try a professional life in music. 'We wanted to travel and we thought if we didn't do it then we'd never do it. The time our *Horse with a Heart* album came out in America we arrived there with just a hundred dollars between us to last six weeks! It was a huge adventure. What was important was that we met people like Dennis Cahill the flute player in Philadelphia before he died, and we played with Andy McGann and Paddy Reynolds.' Travelling to Minneapolis, where Dáithí Sproule and Paddy O'Brien lived, exposed them to other kinds of music. This created an important consciousness of not mixing genres, which has been Altan's hallmark. 'This other type of music enhances your head. You know you'll never play it – but you'll understand other musicians, and other types of music.'

Mairéad and Frankie's first album, *Ceol Aduaidh,* came as a result of Gael Linn director Roibeard Mac Gabhrán's interest in their Donegal material, and, a year later, meeting Green Linnet's Wendy Newton with Mícheál Ó Dómhnaill in Milltown Malbay led to another in 1983. This was called *Altan*, the name of a lake at the foot of Errigal mountain, and for it they were joined by Mark Kelly on guitar and

Ciarán Curran on bouzouki. Mairéad's father had already used 'Ceoltóirí Altain' for the name of a *céilí* band at home, but, after Paul O'Shaughnessy joined up, the name 'Altan' stuck, and two years later another album followed. Coincidentally, it is a word that occurs with a roughly similar meaning in several languages, so it was universal.

Mairéad and Frankie met when she was fifteen. 'He was about eighteen and didn't play a note.' He was spending the summer in Donegal before he went to Queen's and just came into the session. Mutual attraction blossomed. Frankie wrote to her 'and between summer and Hallowe'en at Andersonstown sessions he had met friends who told him, "If you're going to be going out with Mairéad Mooney, you'd better start playing whistle or something!" So he got a whistle and taught himself.'

Belfast was a good environment for learning flute and whistle. It had flute players like Gary Hastings and Desi Wilkinson (Crann), Sam Murray and Hammy Hamilton. 'It was a good time to be learning the flute there, because everybody had their own style. There wasn't anyone copying the next person – they were all seeking music from the likes of Roger Sherlock, Cathal McConnell and Conall Ó Gráda, or going down the country. He just threw himself into the music. Frankie was also a huge rock and roll fan – Rory Gallagher, Van Morrison. He never played any of it – he just loved going to hear different types of music.' Frankie's uncle was married to the daughter of one of the great Ulster singers, the Lough Neagh weaver and fiddler, Robert Cinnamond, and Robert was in Frankie's home regularly. 'His memory of him was as a gentle soul singing "Dobbin's Flowery Vale", a version that Frankie plays. And he had all those Northern versions of songs. Frankie used to say "really I have no tradition", but he had a connection with the tradition which he didn't know himself.'

Mairéad sees Altan as 'a successful band who have stuck to what we believe in. And we were like this even when we were fifteen. We always loved music as "the raw bar", and we know that that is the ideal way to play it.' The band's other fiddler Ciarán Tourish and accordionist Dermot Byrne are from Buncrana, Dáithí Sproule is from across the Foyle in Derry, Ciarán Curran from Fermanagh, and Mark Kelly from Dublin. She sees herself and the band as very much of the place where they got their music – from John Doherty, her father, Con Cassidy, Vincent Campbell, James Byrne: 'Those people are so important to us that we would never insult them by playing their music "not right". We're trying to do it through the tradition, but bringing it to a wider audience. They've all given us an inspiration and we want to fulfil that.'

The major economic success of the Chieftains, Mairéad feels, has actually made it easier for herself and Altan to stay 'true to the tradition'. 'We don't have to build awareness – they've already done that. They have broken the ground.' The word 'Celtic' used to describe Irish music she regards as a marketing ploy. 'We play Irish traditional music. That's all we play – we're not "world" music or anything else.' She has firm opinions about 'cross-over' music: 'If you're going to delve into other music, you have to know the other music as well as your own. But if you learn a few riffs from blues or jazz and throw it into Irish music — you're just only dabbling. The jazz musicians will see that and the traditional musicians will see that. So you're pleasing nobody.' When she listens to jazz, it's jazz she wants to hear: 'It's like drinking a good whiskey — when it's a good enough whiskey you don't have to water it down.'

Mairéad learned music for dancing right from the start. 'My mother dances, my father dances. I'm able to dance highlands, I'm able to dance mazurkas. So when we play highlands, I'm playing the dance.' She likes audiences to get up and dance. 'I love it; the rowdier the better sometimes!' On their last tour in the US they played to crowds of approximately a thousand, sometimes at two shows in Nashville, or four thousand on St Patrick's Day. 'We

worked very very hard on that scene for years and years and it's just coming to fruition now.'

An Píobaire Mór once had to stand up to the priest of Luinneach in defence of music and dance. Four decades later, the great-grandchild of his neighbour and benefactor tells his story with pride and is internationally praised for her unadulterated practice of the music he helped fashion.

Séamus Ó Dubháin

BY FINTAN VALLELY

Irish step dancing is performed by tens of thousands of children and teenagers in Ireland, Britain, the US and Australia. We associate these dancers with rainbow mixes of Book-of-Kells patterning in embroidery, crochet and appliqué. *Riverdance* and *Lord of the Dance* introduced fashionable, skimpy dark costumes and black tights, but among non-professional dancers the lavish peacockery prevails. The girls dress like butterflies and, in the words of dance historian John Cullinane, the boys 'like snooker players'. However, all this is hardly a hundred years old, but the steps they do are derived from an older dance style promoted and taught since the 1700s by itinerant dancing masters. And that, in its turn, dated to more rudimentary forms of dance practised even earlier.

Just what those early forms of dance were is open to speculation, but surviving well in Connemara — and in other parts of the country until recent times — is what is known as *sean nós*, literally 'old style', dance. Here is a way of dancing that oozes sheer pleasure, a unison of body and music that is not restricted by rules of posture. Dancers weave, throw their arms about like jivers, swing their hips like belly dancers, study their feet intently and often barely lift them off the floor as if trying to break a magnetic bond. They become a fluid, rhythmic interpretation of the music's lift and ornament. The Oireachtas each year is where it is seen to best advantage and where the people of Connemara strut it on stage and in private to robust, shoulder-twitching accordion reels.

Séamus Ó Dubháin is one of *sean nós* dancing's major figures; so too is his sister Nóra. Gaelic-speaking – born at Callafeenish, Casla, in Connemara, tucked away out of sight of microchip Ireland in a place inhospitable to Celtic tigers and rational ladder-climbing – the Ó Dubháins have been involved with *sean nós* since childhood. 'I seen it from the time I was in the cradle! The very minute I opened my eyes I seen the *sean nós* dancing being produced – in the house where I was reared,' says Séamus. 'The dancing was really born into being like that, along with the music. I had no hassle learning how to lift the leg and throw a few steps.' It was the men who danced it, his father and uncles in Carna. 'My uncle was a great dancer – Joe Ó Dubháin. And, you see, on my mother's side then, from the Aran Islands, they were nice dancers. My uncle Darach was a nice dancer – from Inis Mór.'

Born in 1948, Séamus recalls that in his younger years every second house had a radio. 'Sure, Jaysus, I used to be mad about *Céilí House*! I often saw my father, Lord have mercy on him, listening to *Dinjo* (*céilí* dance music programme with dancers). There may be kids and loads of noise – but he'd have his ear stuck onto the side of the wireless! It was a big thing to be listening to music coming out of the wireless.' In Séamus's childhood, music was made on accordions and tin whistles and, if none were available, 'do you know, I'd often dance to lilting too. After a couple of lads would come out of the pub, somebody would start diddling. You'd hop on from the middle of the road and

dance a few steps so. That's the way it used to go with me, anyways.'

The 'hooley house' is how Séamus describes in English where the *craic* was. 'You'd see everybody trying to get ready for the night. The cakes would be baked, your mam cleaning up and your dad trying to be polishing up things ready for the bit of *rírá*. And that would go on till all hours of the morning.' But even then the children were sent to bed, and as a child he remembers watching and listening at the keyhole, picking up the tunes, memorising the shape of the steps. There wasn't just dance either, for he recalls that nearly everybody would sing too. 'You'd see, between dancing and singing and playing, that would go on till all hours of the morning. Two or three, or maybe four. And a lot of men would take the young girls, the women, put their arms around them and walk out the door with them – and God knows what would happen from that!' The occasion might be an American wake (someone emigrating), but they didn't need an excuse: 'A lot of houses would have music – especially in the winter time. They would have music in the house nearly every week – it might be Wednesday or a Saturday or Sunday.'

Costume was never worn for the dancing, and the standard repertoire of group and social dances common to the rest of the country were done also: 'Set dancing, "Stack of Barley", round the house and mind the dresser.' Solo step dance was always called *sean nós* in his memory. 'You would hear the old people saying "déan caper damhsa" – do a few steps.' Organised *céilí* dancing in halls gradually put a stop to house-dances, and memories linger of the previous generation's experiences with the clergy's efforts to eliminate occasions of debauchery. 'They say that the priests often came into houses where there was people playing music and having *rírá* and they used to catch the accordion and take it off whoever was playing it and jump on it in the middle and make smithereens out of it and throw it in the fire. And they used to say it out from the altar that he was the divil. Faith, and they wouldn't get away with that now, for sure!'

Séamus has been dancing since he was a toddler. In his mid-teens he went to England, living in Woolwich and going out to the Irish music scene of the 1960s. He danced often. 'Ah faith, then I did! And plenty of it! When you'd have your 'nough of porter down, a few steps would be no trouble!' He worked at building, shuttering and tunnels, and his society was the tough Irish of those years. 'If I knew my prayers as well as I knew the pubs! Peckham, New Cross – the New Cross Inn and all around there. Back Woolwich – the Rose and Crown. And up around there where the music used to be – Old Kent Road – there was no shortage of pubs. Music in nearly every one of them, especially Saturday and Sunday.' Visiting musicians from Ireland were scarce then – Joe Burke would sometimes pass through – but Connemara people living locally made their own music. 'They would be playing away for themselves. Nothing would be organised.'

Séamus would visit home a couple of times a year, summer and winter, depending on the need or the work. He got married there, and spent ten years or so 'deep in the heart of London town'. He has never taught dancing as such, 'but you'd want to have a lot of patience to teach. It's all right when there's a couple of them – but when there'd be twenty, thirty people? I said to myself it wouldn't be the job for me!' He has taught his own children, all of whom have absorbed 'the gimp' impressively, but he doesn't believe in putting pressure on them. One of his first performances in public was with Michael O'Neill from Letterfrack when they won a Slógadh award in Clare. Comhaltas then invited him on their tours abroad. 'I worked and played all around many parts of America – Jimmy McGreevy, and Tansey and Tony MacMahon – the States and Europe and England. It was the time of my life!' The years filled with the roar of machinery and building sites blend with chunky accordion, the slap of leather soles on cement and lino, the approving, animated exuberance of spectators; the flights, sea journeys, trains and taxis, strange houses, hotels and big stages and laughing people.

His legs badly injured in a car accident, Séamus looks back philosophically now. 'When I was nine years I was hoping that I'd finish school at the age of fourteen. And then when I was finished school all I was dying for was to get up to twenty. But the very minute you pass twenty years, I tell you something, they're going like water off a duck!' In England there were always a few pounds in the pocket, but back home things could be very tight. Up to the day before his accident he was keeping things going pleasantly with dance, and was preparing to head for the Leeds Irish Centre. 'Really and truly, when you look at it, it's the only thing that will keep you alive too – the music.'

On Comhaltas tours his dancing was set off by the costumed step dancers, the old and the new. 'I was like something else in between them. I was in the centre and they used to be doing their thing all around me. I used to enjoy it and it seemed to be going down great with the people abroad and all over Europe. But "the legs in the air" as they called it – it's nothing at all compared to the old *sean nós* dancing. An old *sean nós* dancer, it's not that he dances, but he moves every part. I would work my body along with my feet, because every part of you is moving with the old *sean nós*. With the "legs in the air" you're only standing up straight and you have your hands down and you're looking straight, and you wouldn't smile if the divil would fart!' He feels a dancer should be out there enjoying what they are doing, and knowing what makes it special for them. 'You'd be looking forward to them little tips that you do.'

In his younger days he didn't just stick to the traditional. 'Wobbling like a duck! I was pretty handy with it too. Jiving and rock and roll – there was plenty of it here when I was growing up. We had a little dance-hall back there in Cill Chiaráin and there was another one in Carna – they were run by the priests. There used to be a lot of *craic* and a lot of people playing the "Siege of Ennis", and then they started taking in the big show bands – Joe Dolan and the likes of them – Jeez, there was many the night he'd play back there in Carna; himself and his little white suit!' Times have changed, and side by side with the *sean nós* in Connemara now is the ubiquitous music machine. 'They're into discos now – worse than anything! Faith, then – in the name of Jesus Christ, it's unbelievable – you'd go down there to Carna and all you'd see is heads going up and down and lights flashing around and nobody knows what's happening. Jesus, one night I was there in Carraroe – I was in there and I was dying for somebody to come and take me out of it!'

His touring in America brought him in contact with Michael Flatley, and last year he shared a phone-in with him on Eamon Dunphy's Radio Ireland programme. 'I'd love to be able to move myself like that, but you'd want to be a snake! He puts an odd bit of the *sean nós* into it too – the hands, and that. And I wonder who did he get that from?' Séamus has danced too for piper Seán McKiernan on Tony MacMahon's *Pure Drop* series for RTE.

Séamus's father played accordion and whistle too. His area still has plenty of musicians today, and he remembers Feenish Island where 'nearly everybody that was ever reared there was able to play or sing and dance'. Séamus was a *sean nós* singer too in his time, and took part once in the Oireachtas. Adjudication, he feels, is difficult, and he refuses on principle to judge *sean nós* dance. 'That's one thing I wouldn't do. You'd make more enemies than friends!

It's hard on the man that's judging them and awful rough on people that you know.'

His wife Elizabeth runs the home, and their children all dance and play – whistle, flute and accordion, like Séamus – with a wild, throbbing energy. Connemara accordion style is as engaging of every part of the body as is *sean nós* dance. The pace is frighteningly brisk. 'Miss McCloud' and 'The London Lasses', played on Séamus's Paolo Soprani accordian, yield a rhythm drawn from somewhere far back in his mind. He closes off the visual world and lets the lift in the melody be camshaft to his arms and trip his fingers. Searching for the moment to begin dancing, his son and daughter withdraw from consciousness, almost into trance, and wait for their crest, then move off on their wave in a glorious, mesmerising abandonment. The music is not just in service to dance, the music is the dance – the dance is music. Séamus Ó Dubháin transforms notes and step into hair-raising spirituality.

Johnny O'Leary

BY CHARLIE PIGGOTT

Sliabh Luachra ('the mountain of the rushes') refers to a wild mountainy area on the Cork/Kerry border northeast of Killarney town, a place which has yielded up some of our finest Irish poetry and music. The heart of this region roughly covers a ten-mile wide stretch running from Rathmore in the south to Brosna in the north, encapsulating the villages of Knocknagree, Scartaglen, Gneevguilla and Ballydesmond. Scattered across its rolling hills, criss-crossed by mountain streams, lives a hardy, gregarious people who pay homage to the polka and slide.

Some five hundred years ago, this region was relatively unpopulated until many 'dispossessed Irish' took refuge and settled here. Before Sliabh Luachra acquired its musical reputation, the great Munster poets Aogán Ó Rathaille and Eoghan Rua Ó Súilleabháin practised their craft and lie buried here. But, within living memory, the name of Pádraig O'Keeffe, master musician, composer and teacher, comes to the fore. It was principally through teaching that Pádraig passed on his musical knowledge and among his many pupils were Johnny and Paddy Cronin, Dennis 'The Weaver' Murphy and his sister Julia Clifford, John Clifford and Johnny O'Leary.

Tradition is strong here. Johnny O'Leary, one of those rare individuals who both treasures and is willing to part with his inherited share, can still be heard flaking out his old mountainy music. Sliabh Luachra people spend much time creating or relating stories and tales, or engaging in music and dance to satisfy their fun-loving nature. Musical ability is paralleled by a keenly sharpened wit.

Johnny was born in Maulykeaveane near Gneevguilla in 1924, close to the home of the legendary blind fiddle player Tom Billy Murphy who taught his uncle Dan O'Leary. Other cousins, who emigrated to America, later formed the well-known O'Leary's Irish Minstrels and performed and recorded around the Boston area. Johnny's instrument of choice was a ten-key melodeon, later graduating to a C♯D two-row button accordion. Primarily self-taught, he immersed himself in the hearty music of the great Sliabh Luachra fiddle players.

On coming of age (some twelve years old) he acquired his own bicycle and set out regularly to play at Tady Willie's Hall in Gneevguilla with Dennis Murphy. 'And I got a fierce fright one night. I was going down the fall of ground and I had the accordion tied up on my back and I struck the thing on the road. And I falling, I caught the hairy thing. What was he but a blasted donkey with his backside out in the road. He nearly killed me. I hit the ditch on the other side and I hurted my shoulder with him. That's the first throw I got off the bike.'

Johnny spent most of forty years in duet partnership with his colleague Dennis Murphy, until Dennis's death in 1974. House and thrasher dances, Tady Willie's in Gneevguilla and, in later years, Dan Connell's in Knocknagree — days and nights of polkas, slides, polka sets, yarns and joviality. He enjoyed travelling out to Kenmare, where they danced a different set. 'Our set now, in Knocknagree, like, is three polkas, a jig and a polka, and a slide and a hornpipe or maybe a reel if you like. There are six parts in it. But in Kenmare there are only four short parts. The set would only hold about seven minutes. No bother in the world — easier to play. And the west Kerry set is a long set too. There are five long polkas in that and a slide in the finish.'

For some peculiar reason, polkas and slides are played in the extreme southern counties in a manner not found in any other region of Ireland. They seem crafted to perfection. I remember once playing at a session in the company of the Galway tin-whistle player Máirtín Flood, who, on hearing a slide, immediately jumped to his feet, raising his outstretched arms aloft not unlike the prophets of old, and exclaiming 'Ah, Munster!' He knew — and, in a single gesture, portrayed his understanding of the majestic expression found in Sliabh Luachra polka and slide music. Like dreams within dreams, internal rhythms appear to dance with outer rhythms. Older players like Pádraig O'Keeffe and Tom Billy Murphy liked to play this music at a much slower pace than today's playing. They took their time, and time in abundance they certainly had.

With the advent of radio, the fame of Pádraig and his pupils spread and music collectors, musicians and folklorists flocked to the area in great numbers: Séamus Ennis, Ciarán Mac Mathúna, Seán Ó Riada, Willie Clancy and Paddy Killoran — an endless stream. The Welsh poet

Dylan Thomas, Séamus Ennis and Dennis Murphy are reputed to have spent a fortnight roaming the countryside together around this time and Séamus Ennis was the first one to record Johnny O'Leary's music for radio. During his first visit, he called to the home of Dennis Murphy:

'Dennis had an old thatched house, two rooms and a kitchen, like 'twas nearly everywhere that time. And Séamus Ennis came down. He was the first man to come down. 'Twas the late fifties, I'd say. And Dennis had told me he was coming and I was above and I had a small DD♯ accordion. 'Twas beautiful with the fiddle. And Dennis's father was alive and mother. And in the old houses where the fireplace was, there'd be a hole on each side of the hob for putting in tea and soda and things to keep them dry. And there was a bit of a curtain to pull across, like. So Séamus Ennis looked at Dennis's father above and he says, "Mr Murphy, what about yourself to play a tune?", "God forgive me, I will."

'He put back his hand and he pulled the curtain and took out his tin whistle and there was a cobweb about a foot long hanging out of it. And Séamus made a dive to take it off. "One minute sir, Mr Murphy, and I'll get that off." "What is it? A cobweb? Oh, let that there. It'll only make the music sweeter." Well, he played some handsome music. Séamus Ennis was delighted. He used to play with the fife-and-drum band in Lisheen, you see. He was a great player.'

Another frequent visitor to the region was the Milltown Malbay piper Willie Clancy, who formed a lasting friendship with Pádraig O'Keeffe. 'Himself and Willie Clancy, if you heard the two of them together, the two of them were well met for each other. You wouldn't meet the likes of them. 'Twas brilliant. Willie was down here with us many times. That's why I always go to the Willie Clancy summer school. I never missed it. But Willie used to come down to Dennis's house now and we used go away playing around the place. Up to meet Pádraig. He used die at Pádraig, he used die laughing at him. If you heard the two of them talking, you'd split. They had great jokes. Pádraig was delighted one evening, Willie landed up. He wanted three polkas and a slide. Pádraig went down to the counter and he asked Jack Lyons' wife for a pen and paper. Here he was humming – he didn't bother with the fiddle. Dots and dashes, you know, doing them. He handed it over to Dennis who played them for Willie Clancy, not a fraction out, boy. No bother in the world. Willie pulled a fiver out of the wallet and stuck it into Pádraig's top pocket. First fiver I ever saw in my life, he said to me. Whether 'twas or not . . .!'

Sliabh Luachra, noted for its fiddle players, features the free-reed instruments accordion and concertina to a lesser degree. Pádraig O'Keeffe's sisters played concertinas and also Cuz Teehan, known for his slide and polka compositions. Another character and concertina player, Mickín Dálaigh, possessed many local tunes (including 'The Bicycle', a kind of slip slide, often performed for dancing by Johnny O'Leary). 'He never married. He was living alone above in a long zinc house and we used often be back with him from the hall. And he'd open the door, a padlock on a chain you know – "Are you up there, Peggy?" – letting on that she was inside before him! He followed Dennis Murphy and Julia Clifford around everywhere. He was all music.'

Johnny O'Leary's neighbour, fiddle player and teacher Tom Billy Murphy, handed down some fine tunes. He and another great Sliabh Luachra fiddle player, Din Tarrant, both lie buried in Ballydesmond churchyard, fittingly watched over by the sloping Paps of Danu on the south-western horizon. An invalid and blind, Tom Billy travelled the mountainous byways with the aid of a donkey. 'I asked him one day how he was able to make out certain places. "No problem in the world," he says, "the sound of the donkey." He had two ears. I'll tell you, he wasn't deaf. He was deadly altogether with the two ears; he'd hear anything. And he'd take on any one of them and play the fiddle. 'Twas a gift he had and he used teach them.'

Tom Billy gave much of his music to Pádraig O'Keeffe. Although Pádraig was born in Glountane, he lived for some time at Doon, where he came under the musical influence of his uncle, Cal Callaghan. The musical lineage, from itinerant fiddle player Timothy O'Grady to Pádraig through Cal's playing, is well documented but, interestingly, Cal spent thirty years of his life in the mid-1800s working in Ohio, where he associated with Highland and Shetland fiddle players in the large Scottish communities living there. No doubt, Pádraig in his youth would have listened to this music, which may account for a proportion of Scottish tunes in many Sliabh Luachra repertoires. Scottish melodies are also apt to appear in areas with a strong fife-and-drum band tradition.

Though a schoolteacher by profession, Pádraig spent his days roaming the villages of Sliabh Luachra employing an innovative notation system of his own adaptation for teaching purposes. He loved reel playing and was a master at slow airs: wild, haunting and plaintive at their best. Never having married, his fiddle was constantly referred to as 'the missus' and, according to Johnny, 'when the tunes were going, well he'd say she was really purring'.

Possessing a lively, outgoing personality and an inherited local style of playing, Johnny O'Leary is regularly invited to perform at concerts and festivals and has recently ventured to America, where the polka is achieving popularity due to a revival of set dancing. His tune repertoire is vast, accumulated over 70 long years from the Sliabh Luachra tradition. Like his endless store of yarns, many were picked up in the company of Pádraig O'Keeffe.

In Irish traditional music, a majority of tunes consist of two parts, the second of which is commonly referred to as 'the turn'. Johnny and Pádraig were one evening in the company of another pupil who played the first part of a tune five times, failing, due to a nervous disposition, to turn it. 'If you carry it out in the yard, you might have more way to turn it!' exclaimed Pádraig.

His health declining, and sensing that he was

approaching the headland, Pádraig in his seventies was admitted to St Catherine's Hospital in Tralee. Towards the end, Johnny O'Leary sat at the great musician's bedside, where he was made privy to a piece of musical eccentricity the master had been engaged in; the last of many witty, intelligent and entertaining conversations between teacher and pupil was played out.

'You know two great reels,' he said. 'Don't ever forget them.'

'What are they?' said I.

'"Miss McCloud" and "Rolling in the Ryegrass",' he said.

'You see, "Miss McCloud" is a great reel,' he said, 'but we're playing it wrong.'

'How do you mean it?' says I.

'I'm at it now,' he says, 'but I suppose I won't be left live to do it — play it backwards. And,' he says, 'you'll never in your life hear a nicer reel.'

Whether 'tis right or not, I don't know. He was just going to do it when he died. He said he had a sister that had the first part of it done backwards with a concertina and, Pádraig said, 'twas double nicer than the way we're playing it. He was a genius, you know. He was a genius.

Peadar O'Loughlin

BY CHARLIE PIGGOTT

I have in my possession an old black-and-white photograph portraying a flute player, an accordion player and a fiddler, taken in Ennis in 1954. The setting was Touhey's Bar, the musicians Peadar O'Loughlin, Joe Cooley and Tom Eustace and the occasion Joe Cooley's American wake. By all accounts, it was a great night, but not without its underlying sadness. Cooley sailed the following day from Cóbh, bound for New York; friends and relations gathered on the quayside 'wavin', wavin', wavin'' until the boat receded through the harbour's mouth to veer westward into the open Atlantic. The despondent followers nestled into Seán Reid's Morris Minor and headed north for Touhey's Bar to resume their music making and drown their sad loss.

Throughout the early 1950s, Touhey's Bar resounded to the music of Joe Cooley's accordion. He was often joined by his friend Peadar O'Loughlin, both musicians having the greatest respect for the other's music. 'Joe was always very funny. He had funny ways about him,' Peadar recalls. Years later, when returning to America after a visit, Cooley stood on the tarmac at Shannon airport in jovial mood. '"Now, if this fella [the pilot] doesn't conduct himself," Joe would say, "I'll make him come back and do it all over again, you know." But didn't the plane run into some trouble and they had to come back and do it all over again! He was a great character.'

Peadar, who plays flute, fiddle and uilleann pipes equally well, was born in 1929 in the townland of Cullen in Kilmaley, County Clare, six miles west of Ennis. His lifelong love for traditional music was inherited from his father, a well-known local fiddle, flute and concertina player. Peadar's reflections on growing up around Kilmaley are studded with references to music, musical instruments, itinerant musicians and famous fiddle players. Mrs Galvin from Moyasta in west Clare was among his father's favourites. 'He thought that there was no one in the world could play a fiddle, only her, or as good as her anyway. And I knew her later and I figured out he was right there too. The last time I heard her playing, 'twas great. We went back, myself and Seán Reid, to the house to record her. There was none of these modern battery recorders. And they had no electricity. So we didn't record her at all, but she played all night. 'Twas mighty fiddling.'

The difficulties experienced by families during hard times meant that little attention was paid to younger members who showed an interest in music. Peadar grew up 'only going to hide with the instrument back in the room somewhere and trying to do the best you could with it'. The ones who absorbed the music and allowed it to flow naturally became proficient – the next generation to hold the tradition. During his teenage years, playing for set dances provided the main outlet for expression in traditional music.

The practice of group playing was unheard of, a peculiar feature in the Kilmaley area which may have been widespread at one time. Individuals danced to a solo performer or to those gifted with the dying art of *portaireacht*

or mouth-music. He remembers the night, which in all probability led to the formation of the local Fiach Rua Céilí Band, when musicians first tried to play together. 'People around here at that time weren't playing much together and there was a great character here, Mickey Hanrahan. He was a singer and a wit. He was a flute player and he came into a dance back here one night in a house and for the first time there was about four of them made an attempt to play together, you know. And he came in and he said: "Ah boys, ye're going to rise to fame!"'

And to fame they rose, Peadar included. The Fiach Rua was formed in 1940 from a cluster of fine musicians in the Kilmaley area, which included the well-known concertina player Paddy Murphy. They joined the ranks of other Clare bands performing at hall dances, popular during this period. Peadar joined the band in 1948 and excursions into neighbouring Galway and other parts of Clare opened up his musical life. Over the next fifty years, he would associate with many bands and musicians: The Tulla, The Kilfenora, recording with Aggie White, the great Ballinakill player, and performing with piper Willie Clancy and concertina player Mrs Crotty. In the late 1950s, along with fiddle players Paddy Canny and P. J. Hayes and piano player Bridie Lafferty, Peadar recorded a fine album, *All Ireland Champions*, setting a musical standard for following generations. He also regularly visited Dublin at this time, befriending neighbouring influential musicians Tommy Potts and Tommy Reck.

The placname Fiach Rua ('red hunter'), rendered as the unrelated word 'Connolly' in English, presents another all too common example of mistranslation from the original Irish. Peadar says: 'There's a story about Connolly. There used to be a fair there back many many years ago. It would be a small fair, a cattle fair, you know. And the man who bought all the cattle there, the big buyer, his name was Connolly. Now, they called it the Fair of Connolly, and in other places people called it Connolly's Fair. That's how the name came about.'

Peadar's Kilmaley–Connolly homeland, which he refers to as mid-Clare, is wedged between the two great musical regions of east and west Clare. Bordering the county to the north and south are Galway Bay and the Shannon estuary respectively, where evidence of musical connections with Connemara and Kerry become apparent. An example would be the concertina playing of north Clare, which bears a stylistic resemblance to Connemara melodeon music, due possibly to the great sailing hooker trade of turf and Burren limestone throughout the region in times past. The tendency of previous generations to remain in their own townlands helped to maintain local musical styles, but, because of geographical connections, tunes migrated from one area to another aided by dancing masters, journeying tradesmen and wandering musicians. Despite the fact that much of the music in Peadar's Kilmaley–Connolly area was obtained via written manuscripts (the Fiach Rua fiddle player Hughdie Doohan regularly consulted *O'Neill's 1001*

Gems of Irish Dance Music), many tunes were learned from visiting musicians. The travelling player Jerry O'Shea introduced 'The Blooming Meadows' many generations ago, and 'The Drunken Gouger', now commonly played throughout Clare, came from the repertoire of dancing master Paddy Barren, who regularly visited the O'Loughlin household and held dancing classes there.

The Blooming Meadows

Peadar O'Loughlin, a tall gentlemanly individual of quiet disposition, has devoted many years of his long life to music and is seen as one of the most influential musicians playing traditional music today. Known for his fiddle playing, he is also remembered as a fine flute player, graduating to this instrument from tin whistle at a young age. His father possessed a three-piece boxwood flute, but concert flutes did not appear in the Kilmaley area until the 1940s – with the formation of the Fiach Rua Céilí Band – when several were purchased at one pound each through

Crowley's music store in Cork city. It was inevitable that Peadar would play the fiddle: one always hung on the kitchen wall of his home, available and ready for music making.

He was introduced to piping by Seán Reid, his colleague in the Tulla Céilí Band. 'Seán Reid was always interested in putting everyone that he possibly could playing pipes and I bought a little set from him. Then he gave me a set of pipes as a wedding present later, a flat set of Egan pipes which once belonged to Brother Gildas O'Shea. That's how they came – flute, fiddle and pipes.' The pipers who had the greatest influence on his playing included Willie Clancy, Tommy Reck, Séamus Ennis and an army piper named Peadar Bow.

In the early 1950s, Peadar formed a partnership with concertina player Paddy Murphy, creating great duet music. The Kilmaley combination could be heard regularly at *fleadhanna* and Oireachtas meetings. For Peadar, the early *fleadhanna* held a special appeal. 'The big thing then was when we started going to the *fleadh cheoil*. The first one I ever went to was in Cavan in 1954. The later ones weren't as good, they weren't as interesting. I think a lot of that had to do with being able to do things more freely and to meet people more often. We met people at the first *fleadhanna* that we never met before and we met them again only at the next *fleadh* and so on until money and transport and everything seemed to improve. Now it would not be anything new to hear of someone going from Kerry to Mayo for a session.

It's gone like that. We didn't travel. We couldn't afford it and we didn't have money or transport to go further than the parish, you know.'

Peadar is also noted for his philosophical comments and strong-minded opinions regarding direction and change within the music. From listening to his father play in the 1930s, he recalls that 'he was a great player. And I can always remember tunes he played, like "The Floggin' Reel". I can remember "The Fermoy Lasses" on the flute – 'twas a very simple, beautiful version of it, you know. Some of the tunes that are played today, you'd hear the difference, they're not the same. And d'you know, the more that you hear you might say they're not improved either.'

Traditional step dancing around Milltown Malbay was passed down by fiddle player Scully Casey, who was noted for the *draíocht* or haunt in his music. 'He had it in his feet, too,' mentions Peadar. 'He left step dancing after him in the Milltown area. Willie was one of them, Willie Clancy that could do the step great.' He loved to dance to 'The Rambling Pitchfork' and when he played the tune 'in his mouth', as it is called in Clare, he always incorporated the rolls and triplets which corresponded to the dance steps. Peadar understood that when Willie Clancy played the 'Pitchfork' on the pipes he imagined himself dancing out the steps simultaneously.

Although traditional set dancing has gained popularity in recent years, this inter-relationship between music and dance steps appears to have lost a desired intimacy. In

Peadar's opinion, 'dancing today is a flattened out, thought up version of the original. People have no footwork like there used to be, because they don't have any rhythm any more. All they want is a bit of speed more than anything else'.

The desire to play traditional music seems to rise from a compulsion or need more closely allied to the heart than the head. The recent fatal tendency to concentrate on technicalities rather than rhythm, lift and style has not gone unnoticed by Peadar. 'Even those two flute players that we had here, Mickey Hanrahan and Jimmy Kennedy, I can remember hearing them for the first time. I thought there was nothing in the world like it and I'll never forget it. And things of today don't do anything to me. I suppose I was young and hungry that time for it, you know. It wasn't available, as it is now. There was a different flavour altogether, a different magic. And they had a thing from their heart, whereas now it's a thing from the head, from their brain. There isn't the same feeling. Maybe technically they're brilliant on instruments but, as someone said, the tune suffers. I think I would feel safe in saying that music is more plentiful, technique has come in a lot younger, but the music is no better, if it's as good at all.'

Peadar contributes to master classes held each year at the commemorative Willie Clancy summer school held in Milltown Malbay. He can also be heard regularly performing with his friend and colleague, Paddy Canny. Rooted in the Clare tradition, the style of the Canny/O'Loughlin combination gives expression to some of the finest free-flowing melodic dance music that can be heard today.

Sarah Anne O'Neill

BY FINTAN VALLELY

Sarah Anne O'Neill and her brother Geordie Hanna come from the Derrytresk west-shore area of Lough Neagh in County Tyrone. Flat, peaty and wet, it looks featureless to the outside eye. However, the culture and the English language spoken there are a rich distillation of seventeenth-century Warwickshire Plantation settlers and people who came from all parts of Ireland for a nineteenth-century peat project. Geordie himself was as unique as this legacy, for not only had he an assiduously collected repertoire picked up both locally and on travels all over the island, but he also had a passionate love for the society of singers, the dreamy timelessness of song and music, the rapture of transport to another age on the melodic wings of obscure happenings and archaic names. He had a memorably intense engagement with the actual songs themselves — their subjects, their stories, their personalities and action. For him they were full of information and mystery. He was emotionally involved in the art of singing. Geordie died in 1990, a great loss to the music community. Sarah Anne continues to sing.

Sarah Anne was born in August 1919, the year of the establishment of Dáil Éireann and the beginning of the War of Independence — all of little import locally at the time. 'My father Joe had planned to go on the bicycle to the horse-racing at Donnydade. Then I decided to arrive and he never got to the horse-racing. And there was never horse racing again at Donnydade!' He played fiddle and sang, 'and he could have lilted for himself and danced. He could have danced a hornpipe or a jig but he had no "style" of dancing. He'd 'a' danced just on the one spot near enough at the one time. And he didn't lift his feet too high off the floor.' Like many others in counties Tyrone, Armagh and Derry, the sound of the Lambeg drum was part of the soundscape of his life: 'Where I was reared, the drumming would be going on coming up to the twelfth [of July]. He'd be standing on the road listening, and he would tell us how many rolls, and the beats in between.'

She recalls no music at all in her mother Lucy's family, but her father 'sang in the house all the time. Out in the mornings feeding the cows. Aye! An' he would take down the fiddle at night too.' Other fiddlers were invited in on occasions and in those years a travelling tinker-man Bob Welsh and his wife Anne Jane were cherished visitors. 'Bob carried the fiddle with him in the bag, and once my father would see Bob Welsh come round at the turn of the road it didn't matter what he was doing! Bob would come in and the fiddles would come out and they'd play all evening.'

In rural Tyrone, like everywhere else then, things were tight. 'My mother was twice married and she had three sons with her first marriage. There was thirteen of us children altogether — ten Hannas and three Camerons.' No amenities meant endless back-breaking chores that today are almost forgotten. 'When you come home from school we had the water to carry. And we always kept a couple of cows and pigs about the house. We had to go and get potatoes washed and stuff for feeding in the evening — and for feeding the hens — so there was very little time to be learning to play the fiddle or anything like that.'

Healthy bodies had to generate income in that relentless treadmill of 1930s life. Young people began work long before they would ever be allowed to leave school today. 'When I come fourteen years of age and left school, I was sent away out to work — "waiting service" in houses in Belfast.' Home again during the war years, she got a job near to Coalisland with a First World War veteran doctor and his wife and children who had been evacuated from England. Later she worked in McKenna's bakery and bar, 'then I got married in 1942, so then I didn't work any more after that!' With husband John O'Neill another life began. She had thirteen children, of whom twelve survived, and one son, John, was tragically killed a few years ago.

But before and during all this there was recreation too, and Sarah Anne's younger years differ from today's only in technology. 'You had a big bicycle, and you might go to dances. There was Corr Hall just up the road, and Derrylaughan Hall was bigger — a corrugated iron thing with a wooden frame on the inside. Oh, they had great dances. Then there was St Patrick's and the Hibernian Hall in Coalisland. But we wouldn't have got to all the dances. My mother was very strict. I never went until I was sixteen or seventeen.' There were all kinds of dances — modern and old — 'waltzes, foxtrots quicksteps, and then maybe there would have been a six-hand reel in the middle of it'. Dancing was from 8 until 12, or until 4 in the morning at

Easter and when 'the Scotch' came home on holiday each July. Music was made by a couple of fiddlers, maybe an accordion and a set of drums. The footballers ran *céilíthe* separately.

Here Sarah Anne began public performance. 'The band would go for tea, and there'd be somebody entertaining. There'd be a few who would be called out, and I was always one of them. But there'd be great order when we'd be singing. "Maxikelly Rose" and "Carolina Moon" were great songs at the time – but I would have sung anything at all as long as I sung a song.' They sang when working around the house too. Some of the family were in the local Kingsisland Choir: 'Geordie, God rest him, he made all the difference to it. He was loud and sweet and clear.' Among the Hannas there was no discrimination about which songs were sung. 'When any of the priests came into the school I would be asked to sing. And I remember our parish priest, Father Clarke, coming in. Mrs Cullen was the teacher, and she said, "You'll have to sing a song for Father Clarke." And what did I sing for Father Clarke only "Snoring Biddy". And there was a bit in it: "She had one cow to milk and tie, earlie, earlie, earlie O, she lay in her bed till the cow went dry and they called her snoring Biddy O!" Well, when the priest went out she near killed me for singing such a song!'

Céilí-ing was the social pastime. 'People would gather into the houses at night and have a concert out of nothing – it just happened.' Popular, emigrant and nostalgic songs were the fare, learned from the wireless and records. 'A few

people had gramophones besides us. They were expensive. They bought a new record nearly every week.' People got what was new and different: 'Gene Autry, American country song, yodelling, Irish music-hall stuff like "Goodbye Pat and Goodbye Mick, and Goodbye Kate and Mary"!' They danced to the gramophone too, and as children often had to be 'sent for' when they stayed too long dancing at the Campbells' house when collecting milk.

The Connollys had a radio too, and once a week Sarah Anne's father used to call in to hear fiddler Frank Higgins's fifteen-minute broadcast, which was followed by the Austin Stack Céilí Band. Radio Éireann was what they listened to, and liquid-cell batteries were the power source.

And so, social life was a mixture of Irish, the local and the purely popular. Sarah Anne learned what was available around her, in the home and the surrounding area, but sang what her age group wanted to hear. Awareness of the value of local or 'traditional' song came from the outside. 'The first introduction we had to that was Mackle's Hotel at Maghery in the 1950s. They had a big night in the month of July when everybody around here was working in the hay. That's the first time I met Norman Hudson. The Comacs were there – Johnny and Jimmy, Malachy and Paddy. Tony McAuley (BBC producer) was there too – that's the first time I met him and that's the first time we were at a session where there were the ballads. Just music and singing – it wasn't a dance.'

Their reputation locally led Sarah Ann and Geordie

into the 'music scene'. Dungannon banjo player John McCann had taped them at a 'night' in her mother's house and played the recording to Gerry Hicks (singer, songwriter) and Seán O'Boyle (collector, writer) in Armagh. Invitations to other such sessions and over the border to *fleadhanna cheoil* followed. At Clones in the mid-1960s she met Len Graham who had been singing in a competition. 'Joe Holmes was on the go at that time, so I arranged a big night in the house and I wrote to Len and invited him and he wrote back and said he would come – would I mind if he brought a couple of friends? And he brought Joe Holmes and Jeannie McGrath, aye. And that was a great night and that was the first time Len met Geordie.' An American cousin of Sarah Anne's husband John collected all the guests' signatures. The *craic* was so good that other nights followed and put the house on the map. The Comacs were always there and the Haydens (Cathal's family), and blind Pomeroy fiddler John Loughran, and the Armagh Pipers. Tony McAuley made a programme of it for BBC television for a cross-community series called *In Two Minds* – on account of the mix of religions of those involved in the music then.

Sarah Anne and Geordie were well aware that the visitors weren't interested in popular songs off the radio. Yet until the night in Maghery, all that mattered was to be singing. Then, at a 1970s *fleadh* in Buncrana, Geordie was a big hit with Séamus Mac Mathúna of Comhaltas, which led to him doing workshops for the following year's Scoil Éigse summer school.

Sarah Anne is now a regular guest at the singing festivals at Wexford, Forkhill and Inishowen. The songs she sings come from everywhere, some from her father and the house-*céilíthe* – the local 'Brockagh Brae' and 'Old Ardboe'. Her brother Geordie 'was out' a lot more than she was; cutting turf brought him to other townlands, meeting the older men of neighbouring Derrylaughan. 'Maybe he'd have a flask with him and a bit of bread and them fellas would sit down beside him on the bank and light their cigarettes and pipe or whatever they smoked and sing a song – and Geordie would get it.'

The collectors, taste setters and academics had not arrived at the Maghery Hotel out of the blue – it already had a reputation established, for it was one of Geordie's places of recreation and song-swapping. Sarah Anne learned mostly by memory. 'I mightn't know all the words of them, but I would hear them again a time or two and I'd get them. I seen me come home from *fleadhs* and places, and a tune of a song in my head, and rising and coming into the kitchen for fear I'd forget it. And I would sing it to myself or hum it to myself here, when there was nobody here but myself and everybody else would be sleeping, and go over and over it to get the tune. Then I would get the words. I'd get a song after hearing it two or three times. Geordie would have been much the same. I've wrote out a song many's the time, but I could memorise them when I'd hear them; it meant more to you as a song that way.' She has sung on several radio and television programmes, and at concerts, *fleadhanna* and festivals; she and Geordie are known all over the traditional singing world for their style.

When they were growing up, her own children couldn't understand her obsession, but now they have a keen interest, 'although there's not one of them knows a full song – that's as sure as God! And they don't play music either.' Granddaughter Theresa Hughes, however, sings and plays whistle. Sarah Anne's husband John never sang or played, but 'he loved it and come with me to all the *fleadhs* and everywhere, and enjoyed it. My daughter would say, "Ma, you're filling the house with men and women and them all drinking and singing till four or five in the morning. What man would put up with it, only himself?"' At 79 she doesn't know where the years have gone, 'but when I look back, I suppose I have reared a big family and have had a good life'.

God bless ye Derrylaughan, Kingsisland and Clonoe
God bless ye Kellacolpy, Clonto and old Ardboe.
'Twas he who planned that enchanted strand
From Toome to Washing Bay
And he ne'er forgot a fisher's cot
On the banks of sweet Lough Neagh.

FROM THE SONG BY JIM MCGURK OF DONAGHMORE
(SUNG BY SARAH ANNE)

177

Micho Russell

BY CHARLIE PIGGOTT

Early memories of Micho Russell take me back to a Munster *fleadh cheoil* in Kilgarvin, County Kerry, some time in the early 1970s. Having trundled westward to an unforgettable weekend of sessions and competitions with Matt Cranitch, Tomás Ó Canainn, Dónal Martin and other members of the Cork city Comhaltas contingent, it was here that I first encountered Micho's angular-bent gait led on by a peaked cap, hands folded behind his back clutching a tin whistle. Micho loved company and was forever rambling, mingling and conversing: bits of folklore, snatches of tunes and songs, the weather or the price of cattle, always an uninhibited flow. This is how I remember him. We remained friends and musical colleagues until his untimely death in February 1994.

The emergence of the *fleadh cheoil* following the foundation of Comhaltas Ceoltóirí Éireann in 1951 provided welcome gathering places for the exchange and performance of traditional music and song. Micho's first visit to such an event was at Loughrea in 1955. It was organised by Count Ian O'Kelly, a great traditional music enthusiast from east Galway, and in 1972 Micho of Doolin was bestowed with the title of all-Ireland tin whistle champion.

The name Doolin is synonymous with traditional music, to which the Russell family (brothers Packie and Gus featuring on concertina and flute, respectively) have made a significant contribution. Micho was born in 1915 at Doonagore, adjacent to the old fishing village, an area rich in folk customs and tradition. His youth was spent absorbing the music of older concertina players like Patrick Flannigan and Jack Donaghue, and also being influenced by his mother and aunt who likewise played concertina. County Clare has a strong established tradition of concertina playing. This compact free-reed instrument, particularly suited to Irish traditional dance music, first made its appearance in the early 1800s.

Concerning the local history of the instrument in the Doolin area, Micho comments: 'In the old days there was a concertina mostly in every house in north Clare. People saw it as a woman's instrument. A lot of women used to play at that time. My mother used to play it, God rest her soul, and my brother who is dead too, God rest his soul. Packie that is – great to play with. So some people heard me playing and they said I played the tin whistle like a concertina. And another strange thing, how this woman came back from America. She played the piano and the way she played it was different to other people. You'd think it was played on a German concertina the way she played the reel. Along this land, people used to play the concertinas. Their surname was Maloney. The first to play going back two hundred years was a man called Fowler Maloney. He brought the concertina up to two more men who lived here in Lough, the next village. They were Dennis and Johnny Maloney, two brothers. Fowler Maloney lived in a place translated as the "big wood". The first man that ever started crossing the keys, the notes, was Thomas Maloney. He's dead too. The concertina was a very popular instrument after that. The first tune you'd learn on the concertina would be "The Little Sack of Potatoes".'

Micho was blessed with an excellent memory and possessed a vast repertoire. Brendan Breathnach and others have often commented on his contribution to the national collection. His performances will be remembered for their inimitable introductions and, like piper Séamus Ennis and fiddle player Junior Crehan, Micho created an atmosphere around a melody or song incorporating bits of lore or associations of one type or another. 'There's a jig called "The Humours of Ennistymon" and Captain O'Neill in Chicago, the music collector, had only two parts got in his collection. So he met a man from Ennistymon and the man from Ennistymon had the third part. So I think that was one of the reasons that it was called "The Humours of Ennistymon".'

Often his jovial and fun-loving nature surfaced while performing on stage. I remember standing in amazement behind an audience of several thousand at the Circus Krone in Munich once while Micho held listeners spellbound with his introduction to a Paddy Kelly tune, 'St Ruth's Bush'; the title refers to a French general named St Ruth who was shot from his white horse by a cannon-ball at the Battle of Aughrim. As the proverbial pin was about to drop, and having held the assembly captive with incidents from the battle while informing them that the bush could still be seen adjacent to the Gort–Loughrea road, Micho announced, 'faith', that he wouldn't play that tune after all but another instead! It was part of his spell-weaving and they loved him for it.

Carthy's Reel

Although Micho possessed a rich store of melodies and *béaloideas* assimilated in his youth and middle years, his only known attempt at composition (and this, it would appear, from necessity) is forever imprinted on a variant of 'The Ash Plant', commonly known as 'Micho Russell's Reel'. Micho referred to the tune as 'Carthy's Reel'. 'It wasn't composed by me at all, but long ago I learned it from an old man called Carthy. At that time there used to be such a thing on the Aran Islands called a Pattern Day [14 June]. People from here used to go over in curraghs. An awful lot used to come up from Galway, pipers and others, with different classes of instruments. So Carthy was beyond anyway and he heard the old tune from a piper playing it

and he had the first part but only three-quarters of the second part. So when Séamus Ennis came around collecting the music, I put in the last bit. That's roughly the story of the tune.'

Micho's understanding of the tradition bordered on pure *béaloideas*: the spoken native tongue, music, song, story and dance. He also possessed knowledge of country crafts and some of the finer arts associated with everyday life, including herbal lore and old country cures: *bairneachs* (limpets) for cancer, petals of the wild garlic placed in a stocking for arthritis and the sea vegetable *duileasc* for cleaning your teeth. 'In all the old houses that are thatched there is an only weed growing between the thatch and the barge. It is called *buachaill a' tí* [boy of the house]. There is another name for it called "thorpin". If prepared right, it is good for the eyesight.'

Another piece of herbal lore concerns the humble potato and illustrates how this knowledge was knitted and bound by tradition into the songs and tunes. The healing properties of both the potato and cabbage families are well documented. Micho maintained that 'the water after boiling the potatoes is good for your feet and young pigs like pratie water,' the latter detail being expressed in verse.

I wish I had a bainbhín
A bainbhín, a bainbhín,
I wish I had a bainbhín
That would drink the pratie water.

The air to this ditty (now in the Breathnach collection) he also played as a dance tune called 'Is Trua Gan Peata'n Mhaoir Agam'.

Nicolette Devas, in her autobiography *Two Flamboyant Fathers*, offers colourful descriptions of visits by the artist Augustus John and her father Francis McNamara to the Doolin area, attending house-dances and listening to stories and songs. Although Micho was young at this time, he often recalled associations with the McNamaras of Ennistymon. 'A man called – but I remember – McNamara. They had a house in Doolin, you see, and they used to have dances at a place called O'Brien's. And dancing at that time was his daughter, a great step-dancer, Caitlín McNamara, very friendly to everybody. She married a man called Dylan Thomas. I'd seen him one day coming over the bridge. He wanted to stop and have a talk and we were talking about a lot of things. He heard I played a few tunes . . . And he went away. They used to have a small old road where they used to go to church there and so they wouldn't have to go up the main street of Ennistymon.'

Micho reckoned that the well-known reel 'Music in the Glen' was connected with Ennistymon. 'Well, the glen is supposed to be down near the McNamaras, the landlords who lived there at one time. I think whoever composed "Music in the Glen", it had something to do with that place.'

He was ever *flaithiúlach* with his music and gave of it willingly, mindful of the tradition. Once, while passing time on a tour bus, he taught me two jigs, 'The Little Black Pig' and 'The Mist Covered Mountain'. The latter, associated with the playing of Junior Crehan, derives from an old Scottish melody, 'The Mist Covered Mountains of Home', often marched to many years before, around west Clare, by pipe and brass-and-reed bands. Micho seemed to impart an eternal quality to these tunes: good traditional musicians possess this ability to impress characteristics other than the strict notes of a melody onto the listener. He always held the view that, besides learning the notes, the sound and magic of the music also held much sway and had to be absorbed; it was necessary to learn by ear and to listen, in particular, with the 'inner ear'.

Micho's love of singing appears to have been inherited from his father, who was a *sean nós* singer of note and who also sang traditional ballads in English. Many favourite songs, like 'The Town of Ennistymon', 'The Lovely Land of Erin', 'John Phillip Holland', 'The Poor Little Fisherboy' and 'The Well of Spring Water', were either handed down within the family or learned from other traditional singers across north and west Clare. Concerning 'The Poor Little Fisherboy', Micho says that, 'as far as I remember, Fitzgerald over there in Tovaharagh going over to Ballyvaughan – he lived up there in the mountains – an old woman told me that he used to sing it. I got it from a man called Thomas Conole, God rest his soul, and Conole got it from his father. He came from a place called Ballycotton, below in Liscannor. So this man had a lot of songs that anybody hadn't.'

Some years before his sudden passing, Micho spoke about endeavouring to retrieve an old song he once knew called 'The Will of Turlough Pat'. If memory serves me right, the snatches he had were in Irish and I particularly remember the wonderful musical lilt he gave the English word 'Bunratty' which sometimes occurred at the end of a phrase. Breandán Ó Madagáin, writing about the functions of Irish song, states that:

> *Far from being a contradiction, perhaps the widespread use of song — of all kinds — by people in hardship is entirely logical . . . One of [A.P.] Merriam's folk informants said that people sang because they were poor and the songs helped them. The height of humour would seem to be the ability to laugh at one's self, and nineteenth-century Irish people were able to make great fun even of their own poverty. Páidín Thraolaigh Mac Mathúna of Ennistymon, County Clare, was poorest of the poor, but in the song he composed pretending to be his will — 'Uacht Pháidín Thraolaigh' ('The Will of Turlough Pat') — he enjoyed himself bequeathing the broad acres of Clare to his various friends. Twenty-five years after his death (in 1849) it was observed that this was still a great favourite in the north of Clare and the people there laugh as heartily on hearing it repeated as if they heard it for the first time.*

Micho certainly enjoyed singing the few broken verses of this song he could remember from his Doolin schooldays. However, time and fate decreed that I would never have the privilege of hearing his complete retrieval.

Sharon Shannon

BY FINTAN VALLELY

In London a few years ago, outside the Tottenham Court Road tube station, Sharon Shannon's face leapt at me from the billboards. I had seen it too in Italy and America, and it is well known in Spain and in Japan. This is a long way from Corofin, and from the heady camaraderie of warm, good *craic* and music making among neighbours that this accordion player grew up on in County Clare.

Since the 1980s Sharon Shannon has been hailed as the darling – and reviled as the divil – of the new blood of traditional music. She was born in 1968, and, since her teenage years, her radiant personality and compulsive music making have interpreted her as the best proselytiser traditional music ever had. Although she is loved by many for her cheerful, passionate playing, she has sometimes been criticised for moving between music genres – damned by tight-mouthed zealots who actually know nothing about her. But such a young musician cannot be expected to carry the defensive and protective burdens of the consciousness of the 1950s to 1970s 'revival' of Irish music – that has already been done by others. Nor is music a morbid business. It is ultimately pleasant and recreational, even if it is also gravely, emotionally and artistically expressive.

Sharon Shannon enters the picture at a time when the *fleadh*, the session and the gig were all in place, public hostility had dissipated, and music was for pleasure. Having been under threat from modernism and lack of recognition up to the 1960s, by the 1990s Irish music is now seen as challenged by over-exploitation. The young gods of its success have become the fall-guys, and the Comhaltas maxim of 'Mol an óige, agus tiocfaidh sí' has been bitten back as some of the older brigade found they couldn't hear the music above the trampling of youthful feet over their protectively wrought aesthetics.

It was Sharon's older brother Gary who started her in music, at the age of six. 'He went to tin whistle lessons locally in Corofin. Then we followed him. But most of what my older sister Majella, myself and Mary learned – he taught us.' Tony Linnane gave Sharon a few whistle lessons too, and such was their enthusiasm that, when Gary took up the concert flute at secondary school, the sisters wanted to do that too. 'But he had the idea that we should all take up different instruments, and maybe have a little band of our own. So we all picked out what we wanted – Majella decided on the fiddle, I decided on the accordion and Mary decided on a banjo. So within a couple of months my parents bought us all the instruments that we wanted, and we more or less taught ourselves from what we knew already on the whistle.'

East Clare was an exciting place to be for music in those years; all age groups were involved in the social side of it. 'Frank Custy used to run céilís in Toonagh every Friday night and this was a great outing for us. It was brilliant for young people playing. We'd either be dancing or we could go up on the stage and play for the dancers as well. My parents used to go – there were old people and young people. It was a great night out that we used to look forward to. It gave us great enjoyment out of the music rather than a hard slog of learning loads of tunes. We wanted to learn them and to play them, and we've an awful lot to thank Frank Custy for.'

When Sharon was fourteen or so, concertina player and academic Gearóid Ó hAllmhuráin brought the Shannons and various local musicians – fiddler James Cullinane, Carol Talty, the Custys and others – together with younger Dubliners Ronan and Tiarna Browne, Mark Kelly, Tom O'Brien and Róisín Hickey to make *Disart Tola*, a record of east Clare music. Recorded at Dublin's Windmill Lane, that was her first experience of the studio.

Ex-Donegal fiddler Tommy Peoples had lived in the area since the early 1970s and fiddler Bernie Whelan introduced the Shannons to his music. 'I became completely obsessed with Tommy Peoples. I used to always have him in the headphones, and I still listen to him all the time.'

Sharon's father is from Wellbrook, Corofin, her mother from Ballinacally, near Kildysart. Both sets of grandparents played concertina. Her father, I.J., plays a little music (on the Jew's harp), her mother Mary (Garry) not at all. However, they were great dancers. 'There was always dancing in the house, and they'd bring us to pubs later as well. We used to always be playing for dancers – that's how our music is fairly lively. You were always judged on what way you could play for dancers.' For the first half of her teenage years, Sharon played scores of gigs with showband-style groups – with a drummer, bass and singer 'for the jives'. She played for the sets too, and for old-time waltzing, 'and then I discovered Doolin!'

She attended national school at Corofin and Ruan, then secondary level at Coláiste Mhuire in Ennis. The Custys (fiddlers) all went there, and Siobhán Peoples and singer Maura O'Connell too. Young fiddler Michelle O'Brien presently goes there. Indeed, such is the cluster of talent passing through the school that the music teacher has organised an album comprising tracks from her acclaimed ex-students.

Sharon then went to study Irish and German at University College Cork in 1987, a time spent madly playing session-gigs in the Ovens Tavern and other places. She played with ex-De Danann box player Aidan Coffey, and fiddlers Matt Cranitch and Dave Hennessy. 'I made loads of really good friends in the music down there. I was just wasting my time going to lectures, so I stopped, and started learning the fiddle. I spent every day at it – I was completely obsessed. It was great for my head.' Once started on the fiddle she had another outlet in music, and, as well, since she had spent her childhood listening to fiddlers and having learned all her music from fiddle players, she felt that 'that's what's in my heart'. Each instrument has its limitations and its advantages. The hallmark of an original accordion player is what they do with their 'spare' fingers; their personal use of chords. Fiddle is quite different, depending on what sort of music she finds herself playing. Clare tunes were what she learned and played with Frank

Custy, then there were Tommy Peoples and Matt Molloy records, the Noel Hill–Tony Linnane album with Alec Finn's bouzouki, De Danann and Stockton's Wing.

Sharon doesn't particularly think about how she plays a tune; it comes out as she feels it. 'I imagine it's different nearly every time I play, depending on the mood.' She plays a lot on her own when at home, but avoids solo performance. 'I love company and I love the craic, and I love the lads that I play with. I don't mind being on tour when there's a gang with me, but I'd be very lonely going off around on my own. If I had a choice between doing solo gigs or going back to playing in the pubs locally, I'd prefer to go back to the pubs.'

Her brother Gary now runs the family farm, even though he was the first of them to record in 1989. Sharon and her sister Mary playing music for a living worried their parents sick in the beginning, but 'they've come around now. They appreciate that we've a great life, and they can see how hard other people have to work.' Their father was always 'mad into horses'. He bred them and the girls trained and show-jumped them. Sharon still does a lot of horse-riding.

During her time in Cork Sharon travelled up to Doolin, County Clare, every weekend to do gigs. Micho Russell was a great friend to her. After Cork she took a commercial course in Limerick for six months, spending half her time there and the rest in Doolin or at home. With no interest in working in an office, she 'headed straight for Doolin as soon as that was finished' until she was twenty.

Through bouzouki player Brendan O'Regan she did the music for Behan's *The Hostage* at the Druid Theatre in Galway, and, after touring that, 'off I went to Galway, of course, and had a brilliant time! I was humming and hawing about whether to stay there or go back to Doolin, and then I met Moya Cannon [poet], who became a great friend – and I ended up staying in her house for four years.'

She joined *bodhrán* player Johnny Ringo McDonough in the group Arcady, and there were memorable times spent playing with Seán, Breda and Cora Smith at Tony and Phil Moylan's idyllic Winkles Hotel in Kinvara. 'We used to stay there nearly every weekend. It was a great place for the music and for all of us – and still is.' In 1989, meeting John Dunford through the Waterboys rock group led her to try to record an album at Winkles. However, after a weekend that also involved Donal Lunny and guitarist Gerry O'Beirne, she ended up doing a tour with the Waterboys, who were then based in Spiddal. 'Cooney and Begley were with them as well. It was a fantastic time, so I didn't finish off my record. I just stayed with the Waterboys for about a year and a half, touring and recording.'

She enjoyed the new experience of playing with other instruments, 'drums, bass and sax, different guitars and stuff like that. I really got a great kick out of it, and learned lots of new tunes as well from all the travelling we were doing.' Touring with the Waterboys brought her to festivals all over Europe – Spain, Portugal and Italy – and to America.

By 1990 she had a very different idea of how she wanted her first album to be. Her friend John Dunford had helped her so much that she asked him to be her manager, 'because the phone used to be ringing constantly and it used to drive me mad'. The album led to promotional gigs with other musicians, and these developed into a band. 'Trevor played the bass, I asked Steve Cooney, and Máire Bhreathnach was the special guest for the first gig. When the four of us played together, it really went well. That became the band. The gigs started coming in, and it just went from there. There was never really a major plan.' Donagh Hennessy and Trevor Hutchinson, who played with her for years, are now with the group Lughnasa. She has played a lot with Donal Lunny and most recently with Nigel Kennedy, but her own band is still on the road, with Galvin Ralston (son of Kerry singer Jós Begley) on guitar, her sister Mary, and Sligo bass player James Blennerhasset.

The music she plays may include a little of everything – swing, Cajun, French Canada, Cape Breton – but Irish is the lodestone. She is currently collaborating with Steve Cooney on a joint album of their own original material, she has written material with Mary, and has done a set of tunes for a film with Donal Lunny which they have now worked into an album. Most recently she has been to Japan with Lunny's band, and all over Europe with her own group.

Sharon Shannon is small in stature, her personality warm and fun-loving, her demeanour caring and generous. Her sense of place roots her music where she was reared and where she learned it. But stage- and studio-work or no, she still 'couldn't live without' playing sessions and having tunes with friends. The social life of casual music-making is what locates her in the world — a release if she's down, a boost if she's happy.

Roger Sherlock

BY CHARLIE PIGGOTT

An interesting question often pondered on by traditional musicians is why certain tunes never fail to lose their appeal and persist in musical repertoires from one generation to the next. Many of the older melodies, like 'Down the Broom', 'The Bird in the Tree', 'The Old Bush' and 'The Bucks of Oranmore', seem imbued with a peculiar character not found in tunes of inferior quality; an abundance of so-called 'compositions' in the latter category are apt to appear in many modern-day recordings.

The Arabic word *báraka* may hold a partial answer to the question. It refers to 'blessedness', experienced in poetic ecstacy or in the rapture of Dervish dancers. On a more down-to-earth level, it applies to a certain quality picked up by everyday objects, such as cooking utensils or furniture, cared for and treasured over time. It can be said that these possess *báraka.* The Irish word *baile* (townland), in its higher meaning, 'blessed', translates as an equivalent; it is used in expressions like *Bail ó Dhia ar an obair* (God bless the work).

Many of the old powerful melodies can be said to possess *báraka*, instilled either at birth or accumulated during subsequent delicate handling. Countless musicians, among them John Doherty, Aggie White, Jack Coen and Paddy Cronin, to name but a few, have played these melodies, always careful to treat them with the special reverence the tunes appear to command. The respected flute player Roger Sherlock also comes to mind, another guardian of this tradition.

Though born in Mayo (some two hundred yards from

the Sligo border), Roger has always considered Gurteen his home town: this was where he attended school and mass and played music at country house-dances. Encouraged by his grandfather, he played tin whistle throughout his school years, a practice which often caused friction in the classroom. ''Twas something I'll never forget. I used to bring my Clarke whistle in my school bag. And when we'd have a break for lunch, I used to go into the turf-house and be practising there, trying to bring out a tune. In those days, of course, there was no music lessons in the school. And when we'd be called back after the break, I'd be the first one the teacher would pick on to answer some questions. And, if I didn't know the answer, "Well," he'd say, "you know more about that tin whistle you have in your bag than you know about geography," and wallop! across the head with an ash plant. That was the lesson we got going to school on music. It sticks in my memory.'

Roger grew up listening to and absorbing the music of three fine Sligo fiddle players, Pack Spellman, John Henry and Pat Kelleher. However, his greatest musical influence came from local character and musician Paddy 'Jim Frank' Hunt who was 'a very strong, a very wild flute player. He had very old tunes and had most unusual names for these tunes.'

While on musical excursions, the mode of transport of both mentor and novice was the donkey and cart. This was also during an age when many country youths went barefoot, and Roger vividly recalls borrowing his sleeping father's shoes to attend country dances, though always careful to replace them before the onset of dawn.

The age-old farming practice of humans and animals sharing the same roof, though still widespread in many parts of the world, has all but vanished here in Ireland. A story is told about Paddy 'Jim Frank', who 'was known to play in this house one night. 'Twas only a kitchen and a room and there was so many people in it. He was playing up near the room door where they used always head for anyway, because it would be next to the tea. But there was a little door at his back and he had a long American concert flute. And with the crowd that was in it, he hadn't much room, you know. So he opened the little door and he put the end of the flute out the door to give himself more space. And what was outside, only it was the henhouse. And he was playing away and he found himself with the flute off-balance. He looked around and there was a young hen and she perched on the end of the flute. That was Paddy Hunt.'

Paddy 'Jim Frank' regularly visited the famous Coleman household in Knockgrania and, growing up in this engaging environment, Roger gained a solid grounding in the south Sligo/north Roscommon musical tradition which also produced many other fine flute players, like Patsy Hanley, Séamus Tansey, Josie McDermott and Matt Molloy.

Like many of his fellow-countymen and -women, Roger emigrated in 1953 to London, where he has spent most of his life. Here, throughout the 1950s and 1960s,

Irish traditional music was thriving, due, to some extent — according to musician Reg Hall — to the breweries' recognition of the fact that Irish landlords attracted Irish customers. Many new pubs and halls were granted licences for music making. In essence, musicians and their followers transplanted their country house-sessions to mid-London pubs, many of the musicians coming from the western counties of Sligo, Mayo, Galway, Clare and Kerry. 'It was from here that I met all the different musicians from different counties, and you picked up different things, listened to other styles. I met them all, going back': the legendary duo Maggie Barry and Michael Gorman, in their heyday at this time, and others performing around Camden Town, like Eddie Bolger, Jimmy Hogan, Jimmy Power and flute player and composer Paddy Taylor. Roger mentions that Michael Gorman 'composed "The Mountain Road" (a most popular tune) and he composed another one called "The Strayaway Child". The mountain road is a road leading out from Tobercurry to a place called Moylough. John Vesey came from Moylough. He went to America.'

Next to come on the scene, in 1956, were Willie Clancy and Máirtín Byrnes, followed by Bobby Casey. People flocked to the Laurel Tree in Camden Town to hear Willie and Bobby play together. 'They used to play there on Saturday nights and of course they used come from far and near looking at those pipes. They'd never seen uilleann pipes before. And, I'm telling you, Willie was playing well then. Himself and Bobby used play lovely together.'

Subsequently, Máirtín Byrnes, Willie Clancy and Roger took lodgings together in Chalk Farm Road, their base during two years of music making and merriment. 'We had some terrible wild nights there. We used play "The Ol' Bush" and "The Galtee" together. And Willie played "Rakish Paddy" a hell of a lot. Of course, he spoke very highly of Johnny Doran. There again he used to speak a lot about Martin Rochford and Séamus Ennis, whom he knew well. He was crazy about a reel called "Ma Ma's Pet". He picked it up from me, and "Coleman's Cross" and "The Kilavil Fancy", two reels he didn't have that time but I used play a lot. And, of course, he was master of the slow air. I used to love him playing airs.'

There was music in the air: on building sites, in lodgings and in the halls and pubs. If they were not playing music, then it served as the focal point of many a witty conversation. Even those who could not play instruments were humming jigs, reels and hornpipes behind pick and shovel. During a visit to Michael Gorman's house one evening, Roger remembers that: 'Myself, Willie Clancy and Máirtín Byrnes were going out to meet Michael, out to Bethnal Green. We got on the bus at Camden Town and we were upstairs, the three of us chatting about Mick Gorman, Maggie Barry and the music, and the conductor came around for the fares. Máirtín was going to get the tickets. So, with the talk of Maggie Barry and Mick Gorman, the conductor said, "Tickets. Where are you going?" "Oh," Máirtín says, "three to Mickín Gorman's!" He thought the conductor should have known who Mick Gorman was, you know. He was a mighty character, Máirtín Byrnes.'

Roger Sherlock and accordion player Kit O'Connor, who apprenticed under Joe Cooley, were recorded in the early 1960s by Ciarán Mac Mathúna for his radio programme *A Job of Journeywork*, making Roger's name a byword at home and abroad. His flute playing was greatly admired and included in his repertoire were many fine personal settings of melodies like 'Sherlock's Fancy' and 'The Caracastle Lass'. Séamus Ennis, while working for the BBC on his series *As I Roved Out*, also attended many of the London sessions, often dueting with Willie Clancy.

Like many of the immigrant musicians, Roger 'worked the buildings', but he soon turned to carpentry as a profession for most of his forty years in London. Due to a chance meeting with Kerryman John Byrnes, owner of several Irish dance halls in London, Coventry and Birmingham (including the famed Galtymore in Cricklewood and the Hibernian in Fulham Road), a great deal of time was spent working and shaping bar counters and dance floors by day while music making by night. He subsequently performed in these halls with three *céilí* bands, The Dunloe, The Hibernian and The Thatch, eventually playing for many years in The Favourite in Holloway Road with traditional musicians Raymond Roland, Vincent Griffin, Seán Maguire, Liam Farrell and Brendan McGlinchy.

Roger returned to Ireland some years ago. He now resides on the east coast, still playing his favoured Sligo music. During a recent visit he spent time reminiscing about his young days around Gurteen, about Jim and Michael Coleman, and his mentor Paddy 'Jim Frank' Hunt.

That Paddy 'Jim Frank', he played with Jim Coleman, Michael Coleman's brother. My mother that time in her day was going to dances. And she said, if you were coming towards a house where the dance would be, that you'd swear it was three fiddles that was playing when Jim would be playing on his own. And, you know, coming near the morning, about five or six o'clock, they used take the half-door off the hinges and put it on the floor. He used play and dance at the same time, you see. And that was when they used throw the money in on the half-door. Of course, 'twas only pence, and that was his payment for the night.

Well, then he'd put the fiddle in the case and outside he had a flock of geese that would accompany him to and from the dances. The geese used to follow him everywhere. He had fifteen or eighteen geese. And he used to walk from our house to a place called Drumacoo, which would be — he used to walk as the crow flies of course, across the fields and the bogs — 'twould be roughly about seven miles. And the geese would be with him all the time.

The musical tradition of south Sligo and the Colemans lives on through the playing of musicians like Roger Sherlock. Tunes and yarns are constantly re-born and re-told. Another story he related, before we parted company, concerns an unusual occurrence at the Coleman household on the night that Michael Coleman died.

Michael's brother Owen
He was a lovely man
He was a great man for music
He was always lilting.

This was the old house
The fiddle wasn't there
But there was an old peg
Over the fireplace
And he used to say

There was a fiddle hanging there
The night that Michael died
And, he says,
We were sitting around the fire

It was twenty past nine
And the fiddle let this almighty crack,
For no reason now,
Nobody went near it.

So next, two days time,
They got the letter, they got the word
That Michael had died.
He was found in his seat.

That was in forty-five.
It was Owen's fiddle
And Michael had played it
And Jim played it.

Brian and Eithne Vallely and
The Armagh Pipers' Club

BY FINTAN VALLELY

Once upon a time the town of Armagh was the hub of action for four touring *céilí* bands. Their style of organised music for large-scale social dancing obliterated entertainment in house venues. By the 1960s the bands themselves had lapsed, but the next generation grew up knowing them as the sole representatives of Irish music. Under the direction of the local Pipers' Club, however, for more than thirty years now, the art of solo instrumental playing has been patiently rebuilt. Central to that is the single-minded dedication of Brian and Eithne Vallely.

Born in 1943, Brian is now a highly acclaimed painter, his work having generated an impressive catalogue of scholarships and bursaries which facilitated his travelling all over the island and to remote rural Spain and Morocco. He has imaged these travels in abstract and impressionist renderings of mythological Celts, mountain-top churches, russet landscapes, bullfights, cattle markets, steeplechasing and road bowling. Dominant in his prolific output — perhaps four thousand pieces — is the theme of traditional music. In solid defensive phalanxes his early flute and fiddle players barricade that which they knew to be under siege from both parlour society and consumerist obsolescence. His pipers of the same era facelessly and stubbornly blare their multiple strains in rich ochres and rusts against the encroachment of rationalisation and cultural grey-out. Metaphors for their era, they all protest a dignity for the island's native strains; they eschew modern instruments, confident that they have something of great value which official Ireland is almost blind to.

His paintings today have the same huddles, the same capped traditionalism, but the vast sessions have opened up, the flute is raised high, the fiddle bright with primary colour, the zinc-white tambourine almost ringing off the canvas. Times have changed, the fortunes of traditional music have changed hugely, and this is confidently expressed as a *lingua franca* of casual music making all over the island. The paintings are not only Brian's personal biography — where he has been, what he has seen and what he and his wife Eithne have done and achieved — but they are also the subtly told story of traditional music revival itself.

Like many of his time, Brian Vallely first became interested in ballads, a taste which may have been cultivated by listening to *Ballad Makers' Saturday Night* on Radio Éireann. But in his teenage years his taste in music was Elvis Presley and Bill Haley. Hearing Ó Riada's energising and unapologetic use of traditional acoustic instruments and tunes at a local Gaelic League function in 1959 led him to traditional music.

Studying at Edinburgh Art College in 1961 he was able to get his hands on all the available records of traditional music and hear Willie Clancy, Michael Gorman, Margaret Barry, Séamus Ennis and Leo Rowsome. He learned whistle, a friend in Edinburgh encouraged him to take up flute, and then the next summer on the boat back to Ireland he met Glasgow piper Pat McNulty and some

friends. 'They said that they were "going to the *fleadh*",' Brian recalls. 'I didn't know what a *fleadh* was and innocently asked them, "Would Seán Ó Riada be playing there?"' He took their word for it and hitched to the Clones *fleadh*. Home on holiday again, he and his brother Dara began cycling to a regular session that had started in Mackle's Hotel at Maghery, at the mouth of the Blackwater on Lough Neagh. There they met the Comac brothers, Johnny and Jimmy — both fiddlers — and their brother Malachy, a flute player, and began learning tunes and playing with them.

Mind over matter, the brothers cycled on, following rumours of sessions, players and *fleadhanna*, to Enniskillen, to Sligo, to Scariff in County Clare and Swinford in County Mayo. In time, Armagh fiddler Jim Smith became the chauffeur; Dungannon banjo player John McCann took them further afield to *fleadhanna* in Donegal and concerts in Dublin; Johnny Comac took them over to Fred Finn and Peter Horan in Sligo; and they attended John Hayden's weekend sessions with the Sligo people at his home at The Rock in Tyrone.

By the early 1960s Brian had begun playing uilleann pipes and was secretary of the Armagh branch of Comhaltas Ceoltóirí Éireann. However, a successful concert that he organised — involving Séamus Ennis and the Comacs — raised heckles. Tastes differed and people — removed by a generation from what the likes of Ennis represented — objected to the 'strange' music. Yet, despite paranoia about uilleann pipes, this was not a new sound to Armagh. For pipe maker William Kennedy had wrought there two centuries before, and Brian's father too had encountered the instrument at Feis Mhór Árd Mhaca and its music competitions in the 1930s. Indeed, local Ted Harte from the Shambles area of the city was well known as a player before the 1960s. So Brian resigned from Comhaltas and drew up a constitution for a pipers' club.

Two generations before, Brian's Belfast-born paternal grandmother had been a member of Carl Hardebeck's Gaelic Choir, his grandfather John, a founder-member of both the Land League and the GAA in Armagh county, was himself a singer. Brian's aunt and uncle and his father, John, were all fluent Irish speakers associated with the Teelin Gaeltacht. Another uncle, James, he recalls as 'perpetually singing as he drove us to athletics events all over the country'. On Brian's County Mayo mother's side, her father William Eaton played bagpipes, and sang. Her maternal cousins Jack and Mal Lyons at Bacon played flute; this was kept as a dark secret in 'progressive' times of cultural 'improvement'. Then out of practice for many years, Brian recalls Jack as playing with a highly rhythmic style, evidence that in fact 'the two brothers had played for every dance and house-dance locally'. Their sister – Sister Enda of the St Louis convent in Monaghan – was profoundly musical and taught singing in her school for sixty years, although her opinion of her brothers' music was 'amused tolerance'. An uncle of Brian's mother, Malachy Eaton, once dean of

Maynooth College, had spent his life collecting songs in Gaelic. He encouraged and proofread the book *Amhráin Mhuigh Sheola*. Irish music being out of vogue at that time, Brian's mother had been taught piano, violin and singing.

Brian was married to Eithne Carey of Lifford, County Donegal, in 1969. Her grandmother – fiddle and concertina player Catherine Slevin – was Scottish-born; her grandfather Patrick Carey also played fiddle. Eithne's father Harry was born in Edinburgh, was raised to his teens in Glasgow, and then lived with his uncles, fiddlers John and James Slevin, at Corlea, Beleek. Both his sisters back in Glasgow played as well, but Harry was also influenced by his cousin Eddie Moore, a well-known fiddle player who made a recording as recently as 1996 at the age of 93 for Radio Foyle.

In Eithne's childhood there were céilíthe in the local hall at Beleek, and the family's musical connections were strong and alive. Indeed, Eithne's grand-aunt Cathleen is singer Paddy Tunney's godmother, her mother is from Kilcar, and her uncles, Brian and Paddy Dougan, are fiddlers. Francie Dearg and Mickey Byrne are also related. 'At the turn of the century they all played fiddles, and there was a fiddle in every home in Kilcar,' Eithne says. 'I'm the fourth generation playing fiddle; my children are the fifth.'

'At school holidays, and for all the summer, we would just head for Kilcar,' she says. 'We knew Con Cassidy in Teelin too.' Her national school teacher was Seán Brady, father of singer Paul, who taught them music on Clarke C whistles. Irish was the language of the home, and her parents had songs in Irish too – and they sang. Old-style fiddler Jimmy Heuston used drop in to play with her father, and Eithne herself started fiddle at nine. At all-Irish boarding schools in Falcarragh, then St Louis in Monaghan, she learned classical violin, piano and song. 'Monaghan had a reputation for choral song – it was organised by Sister Enda.'

In 1962 Eithne went to study Irish at UCD, taking part in the Dublin Pipers' Club, Comhaltas Ceoltóirí Éireann and house-sessions that involved Séamus Ennis, Tommy Potts and Tommy Peoples. Through them she met Breandán Breathnach for whom she transcribed tunes for his collection. Friendly with Helena Rowsome, daughter of pipe maker Leo, she developed an interest in the uilleann pipes. 'I got myself a Matt Kiernan practice set and took lessons from Dan O'Dowd. It was through the pipes that I met Brian a year later at Milltown Malbay.'

Unaware perhaps of the significance the *Ceol Rince na hÉireann* collection would eventually have, Eithne, along with Seán Keane (of the Chieftains) and flute player Mick O'Connor, was happy to work with Breathnach for subsistence money. 'He would give us a reel-to-reel tape, we took it home and we got paid two shillings per tune. For me it was a good way to learn new stuff, and since I had no grant and needed the money I transcribed a lot.' At 21 she began teaching in Dublin, moved to St Louis in Monaghan in 1968, then taught music in Armagh until 1995.

The life of the Armagh Pipers' Club revolves around Saturday morning harp, fiddle, flute, whistle and pipes classes. Its other work has been the publication of tutors for traditional instruments from 1972 on. 'These arose out of teaching,' says Eithne. 'Some children were good at learning by ear, others wanted a tune written out so they could practise it in their own time. But sometimes they might copy the piece down wrong, so the idea of duplicating sheets came about, and the whistle tutor was born.'

The first of their kind, the books were a phenomenal success and huge numbers have been distributed since. Three graded whistle books appeared, then one for primary school teaching of song and music, first for fiddle, then pipes. All these and a tune book are still in print and popular. Most commercial perhaps was a commission from Appletree Press for a book and disc set which has been a bestseller ever since (although neither the Pipers' Club nor the Vallelys benefit financially from it).

'The most gratifying thing about our own tutor books,' says Eithne, 'is the number of people who have learned from them – as far away as America, or Australia. They'll write, or meet some of our children abroad and tell them'. For instance, at the beginning of 1998, in the course of the filming of a television documentary about the club, an English BBC cameraman told them that he had learned to play from one of them and still plays regularly in a band. The club teaches actively in its own area, but the books reach the world. A hundred and thirty local children attend classes weekly, and adults come from further afield. Building on the centre of awareness that is the Pipers' Club and its publications, traditional music is now taught in several local schools. Indeed, a quarter of the pupils of the Saints and Scholars integrated school learn.

Through their teaching and books, Brian and Eithne came to realise that there was a need to train teachers to teach the music. 'Too often we have had to pick up the debris of other teachers' mistakes,' says Eithne. Herself involved in the Northern Ireland National Curriculum Planning for Music Education, she was on a panel of sixteen teachers who drew up a programme for pupils from the ages of 4 to 16. In this they had to analyse what was being taught, and look at how it was put across. The results of this analysis she applied to traditional music in a teacher-training course run by the Pipers' Club in 1997. 'The course I devised was spread over twelve weekends. In between there were teaching assignments, things to be planned, done, assessed and reported on.'

None of this has been plain sailing. Mixed in with all of this activity is the other family obsession – athletics – in which Brian and Eithne have been involved throughout all the years of the Pipers' Club. Somehow, too, they have managed to rear five children. Family life and their work has taken place against a backdrop of political strife, sectarianism and high unemployment, all of which are a drain on talent.

Many local players are in professional bands – notably flute player Brian Finnegan's Flook, Leo McCann's Corner House, Brian and Eithne's son Niall's Nomos. There are also many others who are teaching the music. Their Kennedy Piping Festival, held each November, has hugely increased local interest in the uilleann pipes and built bridges with bagpiping. By now, some three thousand people have benefited from the part-time teaching course, dozens of whom are sophisticated musicians. With the Pipers' Club, Brian and Eithne Vallely started almost in a vacuum in 1966, basing themselves around the promotion of a locally forgotten instrument. By now they are known and have played all over the world. Like the paintings, beginning in a hazy Celticism and advancing through to a strident visual music energy, this too is a story of artistic continuity and revival.

On the deck of Patrick Lynch's boat, I sit in woeful plight
Through my sighing all the weary day, and weeping all the night.
Were it not that full of sorrow from my people forth I go,
By the blessed sun 'tis royally I'd sing thy praise, Mayo.

FROM THE SONG 'CONNDAE MHUIGHEO'

In the early seventies, I settled in Drumshanbo for a while. There, I met flute player
Packie Duignan, who worked, sometimes, as a miner in the Arigna coalmines.
However, most times Packie would take the road
where the wind took him — and, as I had a van, I was elected co-pilot.

*I fished the may fly in
Lough Arrow. There, in
a tiny cottage by the
lake, lived fiddle player
Tommy Flynn, playing
partner of
Josie McDermott.
When the lilac bush in
front of Tommy's house
came into flower, we
knew the fly would be
up a week later — if
Tommy remembered to
let me know.*

Years later, I ended up fishing on the trawlers, in Killybegs first, then in Carrick. There I met up with Con Cassidy. Himself and his wife Mary Kate were a great pair. I spent many a happy hour sitting by the range chatting to Con, while Mary Kate ran rings around us.

I met up with Charlie Piggott when he played a gig in Ballysodare with De Danann. Here he is playing with French fiddle player Génévieve.

Charlie and I often went to visit local characters. Micho Russell, sadly killed in a car crash a few years ago, is badly missed by all who knew him. Here, at the back of the house in Fanore, Micho plays and tells a few yarns.

Another great character, singer and neighbour of ours was Peaitsín Keane of Aughinish. Pat had wonderful songs and the best memory in the whole wide world. He would never forget a face. We knew him as 'Come-here-I-want-you'!

John and Pat Piggott live near Glenbeigh in County Kerry. I first met them when
I visited Pauline Bewick, their artist neighbour. I brought Charlie along
a while later and, of course, they discovered they were related!
They are lovely people and I wish there were more like them.

*The Willie Clancy summer school in Milltown Malbay is the best week by far in the
traditional calendar. Here is the best 'teaching' shot I have of
box player Jackie Small ho(h)ning it into them.*

Students of all ages and nationalities troop into Miltown for the week. This young fiddle player is learning his first strokes with Terry Crehan.

It's all in the loose fingers. An elegantly dedicated student of Charlie Harris.

Milltown is very cramped for space. Here, Tommy McCarthy teaches concertina
in the changing-room of one of the local schools.

Early afternoon always sees a great session in Cleary's. Here enjoying the music by
the range is Moya's mother, who had sadly passed away since.
On the guitar is Claire Gough, one of the best players in Ireland.

*Flutes, fiddles and banjos everywhere — the streets of Milltown
are open shops for a week.*

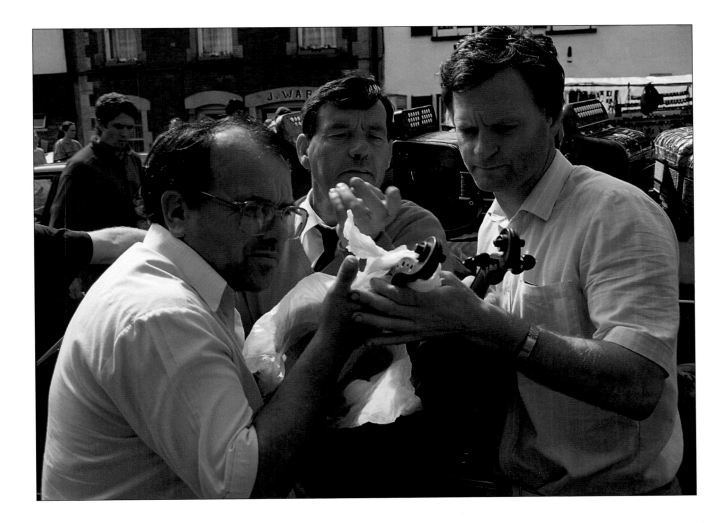

Tommy sells all kinds of instruments and has great patience.
Here, he is intensely comparing scrolls.

Paddy Keenan is a bit of a legend among pipers.
Here, he performs generously for students and passers-by.

Junior Crehan is a legend among fiddle players. He is the chief patron of the school, along with organisers Muiris Ó Rocháin and Harry Hughes. Listening to Junior, you get transported, not only to another time, but to another set of values.

Absent from the music scene for years, Brendan McGlinchey has gone back to his fiddle with a vengeance. Here he is, at a street corner, delighting them all.

*A sad winter morning and half the Kilfenora band and other friends are playing
farewell tunes to their very own Kitty Lenane at her graveside.*

Áine and Connie O'Connell, Ben Lennon and Ciarán Curran — afternoon session in Friel's (if you can cram into it). Fiddle playing at its best. Ben has a unique 'gimp' to his bow — pure nectar.

*Nóirín Ní Gráda.
A wonderful fiddle player,
Nóirín was music editor
for the Connemara-based
Cló Iar Chonnachta. A
lovely friend and probably
the fastest car driver you're
ever likely to meet up with.
Last winter, she came to
pick me up in her Ford
Fiesta to pay a visit to
Paddy Canny. I insisted
on wearing my motorbike
helmet in her car. It didn't
do much for Nóirín, but
Paddy and Philomena
thought it was great craic.*

*I only met 'Big Mickey' once. It was in Killarney. He borrowed Sharon Shannon's
fiddle and played tunes for us in the hotel all night.*

Johnny Walsh is a great bodhrán player from Cork. In the last few years he has
concentrated on his flute playing. Here, he plays for us in my garden
in Kinvara one fine Sunday morning.

Catherine McEvoy is one powerful flute player from County Meath, via Birmingham. Here she is with Felix Dolan, one of the tallest men of Irish music. They recorded an album together two years ago and this is the picture they did not use for the album cover. Felix is regarded as the best Irish piano player in America. Joe Burke, Andy McGann and himself recorded a classic album together, The Funny Reel.

*Paddy Mills, fiddle player and great character from County Mayo. As a reward for
his successful efforts to appear across the length and breadth of this country
wherever there is a tune played, here are two pictures of Paddy.
Here he is with Paul O'Shaughnessy, being filmed and recorded in the streets of
Milltown for an RTE programme last year.*

In a duet with Peter Horan, his Sligo 'energy-equal', in the streets of Tobercurry.

The Lennon family is one of the best-known music families in the country.
Here is Éilís Lennon, in a great session in a back room in Milltown.

Martin Hayes. Another great musical family. Son of P. Joe Hayes from Maghera, Feakle. Martin is now based in Seattle and a great man to put his slippers in his suitcase! Here in full flight in Friel's of Milltown.

Homage to the anonymous fiddle player. I forget whose
bridge this is, but great music was coming out of it!

Wonderful movement, wonderful faces —
set dancers in east Clare.

Kevin Crawford, P.J. King and Martin O'Malley and dynamic Clare music at its very best. Find them some nights in Cruise's of Ennis.

232

A great duo – Jackie Daly and Maire O'Keeffe in Doorus, Kinvara.

A hero — Joe Derrane. If I could pack as many pictures into this book as Joe can pack notes in the 'Broken Pledge' and the 'Contradiction' reels, you would all be broke, as this book would be very expensive!